Understanding Sociology

ELEMENTS OF SOCIOLOGY
A Series of Introductions

Understanding Sociology

Ann Lennarson Greer
University of Wisconsin-Milwaukee
Scott Greer
Northwestern University

WM. C. BROWN COMPANY PUBLISHERS
Dubuque, Iowa

Fitz Memorial Library
Endicott College
Beverly, Massachusetts 01915

SOCIOLOGY SERIES

Consulting Editors

Ann Lennarson Greer
University of Wisconsin-Milwaukee

Scott Greer
Northwestern University

Copyright © 1974 by Wm. C. Brown Company Publishers

Library of Congress Catalog Card Number: 73—92719

ISBN 0—697—07527—3

All rights reserved. No part of this publication may be reproduced, stored in a retrieval system, or transmitted, in any form or by any means, electronic, mechanical, photocopying, recording, or otherwise, without the prior written permission of the copyright owner.

Printed in the United States of America

TO

DEE

Contents

	Preface	ix
1	The Sociological Position	1
2	The Research Cycle	13
3	Designing Research	24
4	Participant Observation and Experimental Design	30
5	Research Strategies	44
6	Social Science and Social Life	53
	Glossary	57
	Index	61

Preface

Our book explains the underlying framework which unites sociology into a single field. From our experience as students and teachers, we feel that students of sociology typically do not know how to read sociology, what to look for as they read, or how to evaluate what they read because they do not know how sociology is created. Accordingly they are also very timid about undertaking sociological research. Books and courses are organized by various topics; very late, if ever, do students get an idea of what sociologists do. Thus they confuse what they read with journalism on one hand and absolute scientific truth on the other.

In teaching the material in this book to upper division students we are constantly told that they wish they had studied this framework earlier in their school career so that they could have better understood and organized material in their previous courses and avoided the confusion which came from courses which seemed unrelated or related in only the most superficial manner.

In response to these problems we have written a book which explains what sociology as a field *is*. We hope to clarify what the discipline is, how various types of studies relate to one another, how this is all social science, and how it all contributes to the scientific study of human society and social behavior. We discuss the understandings which sociologists share and the research that they do, hoping that students will feel they can do sociology. We hope that we speak to and involve the student in the process of sociology.

We have a friend who speaks of the extent to which we professors teach "appreciation of education" in our classroom—but fail to educate. We hope this kind of introduction to sociology will contribute to the teaching and thereby the understanding of sociology, not its appreciation.

In pursuit of these goals, we have organized the book as follows. We talk first about the nature of social science and how it relates to other types of knowing. We then treat the assumptions and process of science. The research cycle is emphasized and the relationships of different types of methodologies to it are discussed. Throughout we emphasize what varieties of social science have in common. As examples of the range of study organized by the scientific process, we discuss participant observation and experimental design. Through examining these methodological approaches in some

PREFACE
Continued

detail we hope to place in relationship and in perspective the dimensions which characterize "soft" and "hard" research and "exploratory" and "verificatory" research. Too often students are unable to make these distinctions and too often they misinterpret them as indicating more or less humanism, more or less scientific merit, and so forth. Having discussed these two approaches, we survey, in what we hope is clear prose, various types of studies. Throughout we are concerned that the idea of solving the problem be central. We use many examples, emphasizing those which have been most easily understood, if not suggested by, undergraduate students. We conclude by talking about the relationship between sociology and other important values and between sociology and human life.

This is a preliminary approach to problems which are subtle and profound. We hope we have not done them injustice trying to make them accessible. We emphatically believe that students of sociology (and of other social sciences) should study the logic of social inquiry in more depth in advanced courses. While this is desirable, we also feel that an *introduction* to these issues must necessarily occur earlier in social science curricula. This is a beginning from which we hope students will know better how to read sociology, how to criticize, and what questions to ask.

Ann Lennarson Greer
Scott Greer

Lake Forest, Ill.

1 The Sociological Position

SOCIOLOGICAL thinking is an effort to map, in clear terms, a largely unknown world—human society. The sociologists are like Columbus, venturing into an unknown hemisphere largely on the basis of faith. They believe that, to paraphrase Alfred North Whitehead, because things are together they are *meaningfully* together.* In short, it is a faith in a larger order than our own wishes and prejudices, one which includes us and is greater than we are.

The adventure is frequently misunderstood. For one thing, there is the matter of words. Sociology sounds suspiciously like *social work* and *socialism.* This is made more complicated by the fact that people who engage in sociological thinking may also be interested in improving the welfare of others (social work), and are sometimes interested in changing the entire society in a direction that would increase public power at the expense of private privilege (which may be seen as socialism). In truth, however, there is no necessary relationship between sociological thinking and either social work or socialism. Aristotle, probably the first sociologist whose writing we know, was not very interested in either of these topics. And most social workers are too concerned with the day to day problems of helping the poor, the old, the sick, to spend much time on what we think of as purely *sociological* thought, while true socialists are usually so anxious to make the new society that they consider anyone whose interest lies in analyzing the old society to be "dropouts" from history.

The slogan of the sociologist might well be: "There are enough people around urging feeling and action: there is a need for somebody to think." And in the process of thinking, one of the first things that is necessary is to be aware of your assumptions—those things which you habitually believe to be true. In short, the sociologists make social life *problematic*. They do not assume that black and white, male and female, young and old, are automatically different in the ways that our friends may think they are. Nor do they assume knowledge of *why* they are different; instead, they question. Such questioning may easily appear to be an insult to the good, the true, the beautiful: this is why sociologists are confused with socialists. They may also appear to be aim-

---

*Alfred North Whitehead, *Science and the Modern World* (New York: Free Press, 1967).

UNDERSTANDING SOCIOLOGY
The Sociological Position

ing at changing the distribution of goods in the world, and thus sociologists are confused with social workers. But their purpose is different: it is to develop a true map of the most important country on earth—the land of the human race.

THE NATURE OF SCIENCE:

The key thing to remember about sociologists is that they are social *scientists*. And we must step back a moment and consider what that means.

Science is a craft, sometimes an art, concerned with knowing in an objective way the general nature of things. By objective we mean that aspect of things which is true regardless of our desires. It is an important and objective fact that if you jump off the Empire State Building you will fall down, not up. (Some of the consequences have practical importance too; we will not solve urban traffic problems by assuming men and women can fly, like angels, and thereby do away with traffic problems.) Social scientists are interested in those truths about society which are similar to the physical law which makes it likely you would fall down from the Empire State Building, with predictable physiological consequences. Knowing social structure, in the way we know physical structure, can be a great advantage to us in running our own lives, affecting our society, and keeping a clear head when we face the "big questions"—those having to do with the meaning of life and, in the words of the Bible, "How shall a young man cleanse his way?"

The scientist is first of all a person with a problem: the social scientist is a person with a problem about society. The job is to find the answer. Creating problems and finding answers is the vocation of sociologists. They are not alone, however; they come from a *tradition* of people who go about asking the uncomfortable questions, "What is human, what is society? What is a good human, a good society?"—a group of people who are organized in groups such as college departments, research centers, and professional societies, and who communicate through meetings of these groups, as well as through professional journals. It is as though sociologists were explorers in some dark continent who keep in touch through walkie-talkie radio. They are never really alone and apart, though separated in time and space.

They are held together as a professional community with a set of beliefs and moral norms which they share. The most important belief is paradoxically a suspension of belief: they do not believe they automatically understand what goes on around them—it is problematic. This voluntary suspension of belief leads them to ask such apparently foolish questions as: What is a family? In answering such questions they go far beyond the common sense, or folk version, for an answer. They think of the institution called family in many cultures at many periods of time, and they observe families with no male heads, with female heads and, as in the Israeli kibbutzim, with no parents present. From all this, they see the nature of the family in a new light. They make the world new by questioning common sense interpretations.

What then are the rules by which they judge *their* answers? In a way this entire book is concerned with such norms or standards. But let us emphasize two major norms or rules without which science is impossible. The first is the norm of *publicity*.

This is the belief that all of one's questions, observations, and conclusions must be available to anyone who wishes to check them against his own experience and judgement. Thus you can never say "I know but I'm not going to tell you how I know." The second rule is the constant *reversibility* of conclusions. The most certain law may have to be changed in the light of new discoveries, new thinking. In short, true science is a study of a tentative version of the truth, not the absolute truth. This is worth emphasizing, for in many people's thinking, science has become synonymous with absolute truth. Nothing could be farther from the truth.

If the scientist is a person with a problem, the next question is: Where do the problems come from? One obvious source is in the problems of everyday life. There is a Jewish joke in which two folk characters, the *schlmiehl* and the *schlmozzle* are defined. The *schlmiehl* is the one who is always there when a hot iron is dropped, so that it can strike his foot. The *schlmozzle* is the one who goes around dropping hot irons. The *schlmiehl's* problem is clear: to avoid having his foot in the wrong place or, at least, *to get that hot iron off his foot*. The *schlmozzle's* problem is to correct his unfortunate tendency; the society's problem is to help him correct it.

Such problems as child neglect, poverty, and the abuse of privilege are problems of the "hot iron." They are common to human society because no institution is perfect, because no society brings up its children to be perfect, because all societies change. And as societies change, what has been acceptable behavior becomes old fashioned, suspect, superstitious, and "barbaric." In a classical instance, for several centuries, workers in the United States were considered responsible for their own safety while at work. Then, with industrialization and the interplay of men and heavy machinery, it became clear that the individual workers could not be responsible for vast systems of machines costing thousands of dollars. Yet they could be maimed or killed when those machines did not function correctly; they could be asphyxiated when the air conducting system of the mine failed, crushed when the corridors of the mine collapsed because of inadequate support.

As this occurred, people began to be concerned with a new problem: the protection of the industrial worker. The solution to the problem included new rules for building and maintaining plants, new social organizations for enforcing those rules through inspection and penalties—including the government's shutting the plant down until it was made safer. With these new laws a new type of crime appeared: the crime of willfully violating safety standards for the workplace. None of this happened suddenly; changes in the basic ways of earning a living created new problems which were (slowly and inefficiently) coped with by human invention. This is the simplest, most commonsense kind of problem which the social scientist confronts: How shall we see that all able-bodied people have an opportunity to work, that children are cared for and educated regardless of their background, that the public is physically safe on the streets of our cities? These problems come perilously close to "social work" but they are genuine intellectual problems.

However, they are limited problems with limited solutions. Solving the problem of poverty in Tulsa, Oklahoma, may be seen as just that. When, however, we start ask-

UNDERSTANDING SOCIOLOGY
The Sociological Position

ing more general questions, such as what creates and maintains a situation in which a large number of people do not have enough money to live in a decent, safe, and sanitary fashion in the great cities of the richest society the world has ever known, we are dealing with a truly scientific question. What is the aspect of human nature which not only allows this to come to pass but actually *guarantees* it, so that a sociologist can sit down today with a pencil and paper and predict quite accurately how many men, women, and children will be living in destitution in one, five, or ten years? In short, what aspects of social structure guarantee poverty?

This leads to the second kind of problem, which we will call, for want of a better phrase, problems of social philosophy. Some problems emerge because our general map of the world is obviously out of kilter; the philosophy we inherited from our elders is no longer an accurate guide to understanding the world around us, predicting its behavior in the future or in other places than here, or acting upon it in terms of our desires. Thus when we discovered that the world was round, with Europe a tiny fraction of the inhabited globe, and the entire planet a minor satellite of a minor sun in one galaxy among thousands, it was a severe shock to a philosophical picture that visualized all of humanity's history as a very recent story set in the Mediterranean basin and northwestern Europe.

And, as we learned more of our own history, our ability to take the immediately given society as representative of what society had to be was shaken to the roots. As recently as Napoleon's invasion of Egypt, we learned to decode that ancient language on the inside of the pyramids and to realize how long and complex our story is, how human beings have built great societies lasting thousands of years and having very little to do with us.

The English are a proud and boastful people, but there may still be read a letter in the original Latin addressed by Cicero to Atticus—a personal letter in which occurs a reference to the purpose of Atticus to buy some slaves. "Whatever you do," Cicero wrote to his friend, "do not buy English slaves, for the English people are so dull and stupid that they are not fit to be slaves in the household of Atticus." In those days Rome was mistress of the world. But even then, and much more so a few centuries earlier, the Romans were looked down upon with disdain by the Greeks, who called them "barbarians," good enough to fight and kill, but devoid of culture and having base souls.
"And there is in Herodotus an account of an old Egyptian priest who, turning to a small company of Grecians, said: "You Greeks are but children, you have no history, no past, no adequate civilization.[1]

Such general considerations are called "philosophy of history." They are another way of asking the "big questions." What *is* the meaning of human history? When men believed it was nothing but a prelude to the Last Judgement and the next world, the question really did not arise. But now that most are less certain, we have such answers as: the full realization of human capabilities (humanism), the withering away of the state and the creation of a society without injustice and coercion (communism), and various versions of these two, as well as the horrendous Nazi vision of the "thousand year Reich" based upon racism and human slavery.

[1] Ellsworth Faris, *The Nature of Human Nature* (Dubuque, Iowa: Wm. C. Brown Reprints, 1971) pp. 329-330.

The "hot iron" problems tend to be local and limited; the philosophy of history problems tend to be global and all-inclusive. It is when the two kinds of problems come together that we begin to approach sociological thinking as it is now generally practiced. When we put the question: Why poverty? alongside the other question: How does civilization evolve? We may answer both by citing Marx's famous dictum that capitalist society needs a backlog of unemployed people in order to keep wages down and enrich the bourgeoisie—the so called "reserve army" theory of the unemployed. You may not like this answer (and it is increasingly questionable in the modern USA, where the problem seems to be that nobody needs the unemployed for any reason), but it is clearly a sociological proposition. It refers to societies in general and it points to the minute particulars—unemployment, privilege, and poverty in given cases. It is *general, empirical,* and intellectually *plausible*. These are three essential traits in a sociological proposition.

There is, finally, the kind of a problem that grows up within a given body of scientific thought—one that might be meaningless to a layman, however philosophical, but which is critical to the technically initiated. Thus a fellow sociologist told of a neighbor in Princeton, a physicist, who is, according to the knowledgeable, almost certain to get a Nobel prize in physics. He has discovered a major exception to a basic physical law— one which would be meaningless to you and me. But his work is a critical answer to a basic question: Under what conditions do these laws hold?

Of course, as my friend goes on to remark, who ever heard of anyone getting a Nobel prize for finding an exception to a major sociological law? 'If we did, we would all be dripping medals down to our ankles,' he remarked. Nevertheless, there are better worked-out areas of sociology where recondite matters such as the role of symbolic interaction in labelling theory, of transportation in the "gravity flow model" of urban growth, do have an importance *intrinsic* to a growing body of more or less well supported theory. Sociologists can and do argue questions of the independent nature of different characteristics along which urban neighborhoods can be ranked and the extent to which psychological learning theory applies in new, emerging situations.

Thus problems come about wherever the new occurs, wherever the old structure of belief is inadequate, wherever new kinds of thought and/or action are demanded. A sociologist of religion once remarked concerning the origins of the soul: "Some person was in a very tight place and helpless. He said to himself, 'Don't just stand there: *do something.*' And he invented the immortal soul. What else could he do with that sabre-toothed tiger coming at him?" Whatever one thinks of the concept of the soul, it is likely that such primitive situations frequently force creativity upon people, whether they want to think or not.

Science may be seen as a body of knowledge, but it may also be seen as a continual process by which humanity extends and revises its collective knowledge of the world. From a given intellectual position the scientist is led to ask questions. These may stem from practical problems, philosophical concerns, the state of the art or, simply, puzzles. After all, vast regularities are wonderful and puzzling. The stars in their orderly movements, the ebbing and flooding of the Nile, inspired certain early scientists to create astronomy and geometry.

In any event, from the intellectual problem the scientist is led to formulate possible solutions. He practices what Max Weber, the great German sociologist, called "intellectual experiments." These take the form "If X, then what of Y?" He then translates these ideas into observable reality, proposes answers, and goes out and looks to see if the world does indeed behave in such a fashion. If it does, he decides that his notions are not entirely wrong—but if it does not, he has *falsified* the proposition, at least in the form he has tested. It is then necessary to go back to his observations (to see if they were accurate and indeed reflected the things his theory is about), and if they seem correct, he must go back to his theory and change it.

If he was right in his addition to the (tentative) truth, or in his revision of it, then the map he started with must be altered. He may have to change boundaries, fill in territory, or wipe out entire states. The process has come full cycle, from thinking about the situation, through testing the thoughts, to applying the results to the original set of beliefs he started with. This has been called the "research cycle," and it is a basic process that goes on in all sciences.

You may ask at this point: Why should I accept his version of the truth? After all, I have my own experiences, intuitions, beliefs. And the answer is simply: You do not have to. Science is a version of truth only to those who accept certain basic assumptions. These are simple but profound. First one must accept the existence of a world beyond his own senses, not completely controlled by what he wishes to see, but knowable in such a way that he can communicate about it to others. Second, one must accept the desirability of knowing that world. These are free choices, but there are good arguments for accepting these assumptions. One does not want to fall to his death from the Empire State Building; one wants to be effective in the real world, to influence and create; finally, one wants the competent response of his fellow human beings.

The alternatives to accepting these assumptions are several. One can act upon the world, but adopt the wisdom of Humpty Dumpty: Words mean what I say they mean. If one follows this strategy he must have great pursuasive power, either through his official position or through his great personal magnetism. On the other hand, one can adopt the position of the mystic, withdraw from the world, and commune with the god of his choice. Without criticizing either of these strategies, I think it can be stated that people adopting them are not interested in social science and there is nothing in the world that can force them to be.

Indeed, it is the element of free choice in entering the scientific game that makes it exciting. Because it *is* a free creation of the human mind based on the human experience, it is an enthralling combination of the mind at play and the absolutely inescapable aspects of the universe which we know. Because nobody makes you believe in science, your belief may be dignified by a sophisticated philosophy, one which recognizes the many facets of human experience and the multifarious nature of the world known to humanity.

VERSIONS OF TRUTH:

The world does not come to us bearing labels, telling us the "truth" of a given event. We may believe so, for we are creatures of our culture, and the map of the world is presented to us with great authority by our parents, other adults, and our friends. This presentation in its entirety we call our "culture," our inherited knowledge about the world. This knowledge may be as clear and certain as the Newtonian law which indicates that we fall downwards toward the larger mass, the planet earth, or it may be as fallacious as the belief that the world is flat. (The "Flat Earth Society" has finally dwindled to a few dozen believers as interplanetary travel has made it clear that the globe is round.)

Truth is always a symbolic system. That is to say, we formulate our sense experience and our reflections on it in terms of symbols, which stand for concepts. Thus out of the blurred confusion our senses present to us, we see a given object and we make it into a symbol, "chair." We conceptualize chair in many ways, but it has a generic meaning which is shared by people in a great many cultures: it is a structure upon which the human body may rest without reclining. It may vary from the sacred "stool" that signifies royalty in an African kingdom to the "shooting stick" which the Englishman takes along while hunting birds —a walking stick that may be expanded into a temporary chair—but the meaning is the same. Then out of all the symbols meaning chair we can generalize to the concept, chair, the structure I have just described.

Out of all our sense impressions, and our reflections upon them we select some as important. We exclude many others. This process of selection is known as *abstraction* which literally means, in Latin, taking out of—as a thief takes out of a house something he values. We take out of the stream of experience that which we value, and we leave behind many experiences which may be even more valuable: we do not know.

How do we decide what to select? We usually do not, for we use the *frame of reference* we have inherited from our culture, a certain lens with a certain focus which shows up some aspects of our experience as "the world." It is by the aid of these frames of reference that we create the fact, which has been called "an intellectually formulated event." We are the creators of reality—but that reality is always subject to check. Remember, we know the world through our senses but what we know is not entirely controlled by our senses. Rather, we are continually dealing with (1) a conceptual map which we have inherited from our cultural associates, (2) new sense experience which is forever rewarding and punishing us in the daily round of living, and (3) our own interpretation of the events.

What seems to occur is this. We respond to sense data by our inherited concepts, turning them into symbols in a larger frame of reference. The cross on the church is not just a geometrical form—it is a symbol of Christianity, and as such it launches us into the symbolic realm where we think of religion and what we know of it. We conceive and *conceptualize* the cross; it immediately refers to a systematic set of meanings (religion, Christianity, Judaism) and has a connotation in the world of symbols, yet at the same time the cross *denotes* a particular religious use of a building. Thus conception is our formulation of the event, connotation is our reference to the world of meaning we have inherited, denotation is the relevance of the given symbol to a given thing.

UNDERSTANDING SOCIOLOGY
The Sociological Position

In everyday communication, as well as in science we formulate experience at different levels of abstraction. We may talk about "chairs" or be interested in them only as "furniture"—a more general, more abstract category. Or we may be interested, like anthropologists, in "the artifacts of a culture"—including all humanly created objects. This is a still more inclusive, more abstract category in which "chair" belongs. Our interest might be, for example, in comparing societies which produce very simple or very ornate artifacts (furniture, pottery, automobiles). Such differences in frames of reference cause us to 'see' that original object differently. "It" is all these things and more.

It is also true that we symbolize in many different ways. As Suzanne Langer has sensitively described in great detail, we symbolize in ways that are quite different from logical thought.[2] We symbolize when we attend a memorial service for a friend who has died; we are *saying something* when we carry the coffin, listen to the music, weep, even when we eat and drink together afterwards. We are affirming the solidarity of the human community in the presence of the brute fact of death.

And when we listen to music we are surely symbolizing. It is true the symbols are not the same thing as $2 + 2 = 4$, but they are meaningful all the same, and people can be fairly sure they have roughly equivalent experiences (though they may differ in judging them.) Then too, in painting we are communicating in a meaningful, symbolic fashion. How else could a European painter like Picasso have learned to so respect the culture of Africa were it not for some basic language, one of the senses but not completely controlled by them and a basis for communicating with his fellow human beings—as in the latter's famous paintings? Whether you like Picasso or African sculpture is beside the point; the main thing is the fact of *presentational* symbols which communicate and have value.

One can think of all these forms of presentational discourse as simply idiocy. If he does, however, he would have to answer the question: Why have millions of people indulged in the nonsense of religion? Why have some of the most brilliant and gifted of the race devoted their lives to producing *Pride and Prejudice* or the Beethoven *Ninth Symphony*? What goes on in a life like that of Pissaro, the great French Impressionist painter, whose entire career was one of complete devotion to his work—and whose work cannot easily be duplicated except through creating the same complex, symbol-creating person he was?

No, it will not do. We symbolize through both the presentational mode (which we have tried to evoke above)—art, liturgy, poetry, music, but we also symbolize through the representational mode in which we try to abstract the logical and empirical meaning of events and make them into precise arguments. These arguments may be as blunt as Henry Ford's remark, "History is the bunk." or as complicated as the scientific arguments for DNA, the "spiral helix" which apparently indicates the way nature imprints new forms on emerging protoplasm, maintaining and varying physical species and types within those species.

PRACTICAL VISION AND SCIENTIFIC KNOWLEDGE IN SOCIOLOGY

One of the forms that representational reason, or discourse, takes in social life can

[2]Suzanne Langer, *Philosophy in a New Key* (New American Library, 1942).

only be called "practical vision." Again, this is Langer's term, and by it she means that combination of inherited notions, the ability to apply them, and the shrewdness which makes it possible for: a good compositor to set type, a good teacher to engage the attention of a fifth grade class and teach, a good revolutionist to create an organization to further "the cause." Such a vision is essentially one that operates by rules of thumb; it is practical, flexible, forever on the lookout for useful symbolic clues to "what will work." This vision is usually based upon unexamined assumptions, but it has the weight of great collective experience behind it. A labor leader senses when a plant is "ripe" for union organization, a businessman senses when a market is "ripe" for commercial development. Most of human thinking has been just this sort of thing.

Much of sociology has also been created in this way. People who want to do good, right wrongs, and improve social health, have seized on the ideas current in the society and launched programs based upon them. They have set out to abolish poverty, do away with racial prejudice, give women an equal chance, and so forth. Their practical vision, however, is incomplete; it was not developed for the solution of such problems and it tends to be very conservative. After all, it is a repetition of many thousands of years of human experience with other situations, and it may or may not apply to the present. Adolescents may or may not "go wrong" for the lack of a mother's love; governments may or may not go to war over questions of national interest and pride. Practical vision lacks theoretical generality.

Paradoxically, science is a process of learning more and more about less and less, for the scientist rigorously abstracts from human experience. The physicist talks about mass, force, movement, shape. He does not talk about physical beauty, grace, or even something so all pervasive as smell, taste, and touch. In science the division of labor is organized by the frame of reference to exclude all that is irrelevant to the kinds of theory employed. In the same way the sociologist is not interested in particular persons—their history, personality, quirks of character, looks, and the like. He is interested in the individual person only as one of a set of persons, whom he then analyzes as members of a group, (a street corner gang, a college faculty, a student fraternity), of a social category (males or females, whites or nonwhites, plumbers or professors), or a temporary interaction unit (street fighters, ballroom dancers).

The sciences have developed this division of labor "naturally," that is, it came about as the most efficient solution to the problem of gaining general knowledge of an empirical nature. The roots of chemistry may be, historically, in alchemy—the effort to transform lead into gold—but theoretically they rest in such formulations as the periodic table whereby Mendeleev was able to rank the known elements in terms of their atomic structure and in the process demonstrate a pervasive order. In the same way the sociologist who wishes to prevent juvenile delinquency may advance **further** through a knowledge of groups in general, and thus delinquent gangs in particular, than through a knowledge of the history and personalities of a given collection of juveniles.

The danger in this process of selective abstraction is great. For we may confuse our abstracted version of things with the concrete events from which we abstracted it. Whitehead terms this "the fallacy of misplaced concreteness." Thus the physicist may argue that there is no such thing as the immortal soul, as he finds nothing corresponding to it in physical nature, while the theologian may argue against the theory of biological evolution because there is nothing about it in the Scriptures. (Whatever his scriptures may be: John Stuart Mill argued, if we are empirical about it, true religion is polytheism since various groups of men have imputed divinity to just about everything in the world.)

Both the physicist and the theologian are making the mistake of misplacing concreteness. Each has forgotten his original decision to *abstract*, to leave out the irrelevant. The physicist would do better to say: 'I look only at matter, energy, time, motion,' and the theologian: 'God created the structure of the world as he would; my duty is to understand God and his ways with men.' Otherwise, as Santayanna says, religion is bad science and false prophecy, and physics an inappropriate substitute for religion.

The sociologist as a scientist deals with fact, as does the physicist. But instead of dealing with the abstractions of matter, energy, time, and motion, he deals with the abstractions of *social fact*. This is to study intellectually formulated events in human collectives, or society. Following the distinguished French sociologist, Émile Durkheim, we may attribute to social fact two defining characteristics. First, it is external to any given individual. Second, it is constraining in its impact on his behavior.

Externality means that, whether you know it or not, you are part of a larger situation which affects you and which you cannot completely control. If you are born at a given class level in the United States you have a very good chance of living your "three score and ten" years; if you were born an Untouchable in India, your odds would be relatively poor. In short, there are external limits imposed by societies, whether anyone plans it or not.

The coerciveness of social fact rests upon several bases. First, society was here before you were. You as a person were inducted into human life by elders and others who helped make you what you are, who indeed helped you conceive the notion of "the human" and "the individual." (The most radical of doctrines of individualism are socially conceived and taught.) Then too, there are so many more of them than you— If you *will* practice nudism on a college campus at high noon, they will more or less regretfully expel you, jail you, or put you in a mental hospital for observation. In short, societies punish those who deviate from custom. Finally, it is important to reemphasize just how much we need each other. The poorest example of mankind would be Robinson Crusoe—and even he was utterly dependent on the wrecked ship and its contents, a veritable treasurehouse of European artifacts which had been millenia in the making. No, it is our fate to be integrally related to each other; we are a group animal, one which achieves maturity only after years of education (or indoctrination) in being some version of human. We spend our lifetime trying to approximate it.

THE NATURE OF THEORY

All scientists aim at a grand design which will explain all of their observations in a coherent fashion. Even though they know they are working with only one aspect of human experience, they would like to organize that particular aspect in a meaningful way so that their theory would explain and predict all the facts about that particular aspect. In constructing such theory, they tend to operate from the most general forms; these forms we call *guiding metaphors*. They are forms that have been useful in a variety of fields, and are therefore recognizable in a more general sense.

In sociology a number have been important; most of them are patterned after work in another science, though they are more general than that might imply. We will consider the two which are probably most used, though the reader can certainly discover others on his own. We will look at the notion of the *social machine,* and the *alternative notion* of the *social organism.*

The metaphor of the *social machine* implies that human beings in society are a set of moving parts in a fixed relation to each other. Each individual has his role (as bees are workers, drones, and queens), and it is a role in a particular group. The group in turn has its role in the larger society. Thus females may give birth to children and raise them through infancy, tend house, and carry out domestic tasks that do not take them far from the house and children. Men may farm, tend livestock, maintain structures, hunt, and fish. You will recognize this role-system in the nineteenth century American farm. Such a farm was in turn a social component of larger groups, each disciplining itself and its subgroups. If one individual deviated from his role, the pressure of others (performing *their* roles) tended to bring him back "into line."

The *social organism* metaphor, on the other hand, is focused much more upon the group as a living unity—flexible, evolving, suffering illness, and gaining health. Indeed, this metaphor, which comes directly from biology, was once considered an adequate theory of human society. Such thinkers as Herbert Spencer saw societal evolution as merely the continuation of the biological evolution that Darwin had charted out for the various species. Social Darwinism, as this school of thought has been called, has largely failed—partly because of its misreading of Darwin's notion of the survival of the fittest which, applied to social life, is a cruel doctrine indeed, partly because of its determinism which implies that human will is of no importance, and lastly by reason of its belief in a single direction of change or progress for the human species.

However, the social machine metaphor is also heavily criticized. It is easy to see that human groups are not planned and created in the way machines are; it is easy to see that many things occur which have little or nothing to do with fulfilling a "function" in the group. Groups are, to put it bluntly, sloppy organizations. They are usually shot full of irrationality, staffed with members who are partially trained, mistrained, and given to lying, cheating, and malingering. Furthermore, the parts may simpy refuse to come to work, may go on strike, may enter other groups through divorce, layoffs, or immigration.

But remember, we have only called attention to these as metaphors. A metaphor only attempts to show likeness *in some respects.* In sociology they are heuristic devices; these are practical ways to create theories that may be completely abandoned later, having served as stepping stones from observation through more general laws to grand theory. As heuristic devices, however, these have been useful. The theory of bureaucracy, which is one of our most important ways of understanding large-scale industrial society, owes much to the notion of fixed, moving parts, in a larger, rational order. While we have an entire profession concerned with the pathologies of bureaucratic order, (management consultants, human relations specialists, and the like), the fact remains that it is through bureaucratic organization that the state, the corporation, the labor union, most churches, and all armies operate.

In the same way, comparing societies to species evolving over time, we gain valuable insights. We see the emergence of specialized groups (social organs) in charge of different necessary tasks, their interaction with each other, and the consequent changes in the society at large. No other metaphor is so useful in understanding history—the effects of the discovery of agriculture on preliterate man, the effects of the industrial revolution, the evolution of cities and urban culture, all make more sense in the light of a general evolutionary theory. To be sure, many of the old social Darwinian assumptions have been dropped. Nobody will argue that survival *per se* tells us anything about the value of what survives; few people believe that societies can only evolve in one direction; few are certain that advance is progress, and most would agree that the evolution is not irreversible. Yet even with these modifications, the organic metaphor is a fruitful one, lying at the base of many current formulations concerning history, social change, and the emergence of new nations.

For Further Reading

Greer, Scott. *The Logic of Social Inquiry.* Chicago: Aldine Press, 1969.
   A much more extended discussion of some of the questions raised in this chapter, this book should be of use to students interested in the general enterprise of social science.

Langer, Suzanne. *Philosophy in a New Key.* New York: New American Library, 1942.
   This is a sensitive and lively discussion of the relationships among science and art, logic and ritual, discursive and presentational meaning.

Whitehead, Alfred North, *Science and the Modern World.* New York: New American Library edition, 1925.
   This classic discussion of the relationship between science and other aspects of human history may be abstruse at times, but if the reader is concerned with the complex fields of history of science, metaphysics, and the nature of abstraction and God, he will find it profitable.

2 | The Research Cycle

THE sociologist has decided on categories through which to organize sense data and has imagined relationships among these categories. Like a map, his theory is only interesting to persons who are concerned with those aspects of reality. A motorist's road map is not a useful guide to a person who wants to know about soil types or natural vegetation or temperature or precipitation. Conversely, a motorist could look at the more than 150 maps in Goode's World Atlas and find no map which would tell him whether there was a strip of roadway on which his car could pass. A person who wants to get across Iowa quickly needs a different map from a person who wants to know if he can grow soy beans there.[1]

We don't ask a map to tell us everything at once, but we do ask that it provide an accurate version of what it does tell us. A map may be partial but it should not be inaccurate. This is a second way in which theories are like maps. If a road map tells us the road is straight and flat, we would be angry to find it curving and mountainous. If a map indicates rich soil or rain, we should not, upon going there, find poor soil or dry weather. We expect our maps to be borne out by reality and we have ways of checking on them. If they do not tell us what to expect, we decide they are not very good maps.

If we decide a map is not a very good one, we may or may not be able to find one which is more accurate. This, too, is like social science. We must rely on the categories and relationships people have imagined to describe reality, or we must imagine new ones which are more congruent. This may be very difficult or quite easy.

Social scientists do not have a 'truth' but a method by which they create their theories, their maps, and check them against reality. Adherence to the *research cycle* is what social scientists have in common. This is not always apparent since there are several stages in the cycle, and a given person or research article is likely to engage only

[1] The metaphor of the map is useful for discussing many characteristics of theories. There is a big difference, however, between a theory and a map. As we shall see later, a theory *explains* regularities in order to predict them. The precipitation map is really explained not by itself but by relationships among such things as air and water and wind. The "map" may predict accurately in a static situation. The theory explains the dynamics which produce the static situation, and specifies when it will change.

one or another point in the cycle. It is important to keep the whole cycle in mind, however, since it is the cyclical process that ties together different types of research and relates them one to the other. It is also the use of the research cycle which differentiates social scientists from novelists or journalists who are interested in the same topics but who do not subject their ideas to this process of reality testing.

Within the research cycle, there is a place for creating categories and relationships from observation of events, and there is a place for exposing and eliminating those speculations and theories, if they do not 'fit' reality. Obviously, both activities are very important. In the "inductive', theory creating, stages of the cycle, the social scientist looks at a problem or a puzzle and tries to explain it. Many people or few may offer explanatory theories. In the deductive, testing, stage of the research cycle we take a more rigorous look at the explanations offered for a problem. We look in the real world for the things which should be true if a given theory is true. We eliminate the theories which do not predict well and keep the ones which does the best job of predicting. Since, in the testing phase of the cycle, we can only choose among the theories which have been suggested, we need to continually generate new explanations in the inductive, exploratory phases of research, lest we be in the situation of having a bad map but no better alternative.

A student of ours once suggested another metaphor which gets at what the research cycle does. She said that social science (or science generally) was like a race in which a number of runners (theories) start out. Gradually they are eliminated until only one runner is left in the race and is declared the winner. He may be the very strongest runner imaginable or simply the best of those entered in the race.

How does the research cycle monitor the process of research? How does it get rid of bad theories? It provides a set of rules which scientists have agreed are the best way of arriving at accurate explanations of those phenomena which can be handled in a scientific way. That is, it is a way of agreeing on the reality of things about which truth or falsehood can be established in an empirical way. An empirical approach, remember, is only possible if explanations can be falsified, shown to be wrong, through observations anyone can make. This can only work if those seeking knowledge agree that the empirical observation provides a route to knowledge. Further, it requires adherence to the two basic norms. Scientists must make the data they used in building or testing their theories public so others can reevaluate the data and test it in other ways. Second, everybody who accepts this scientific position must be willing to discard bad theories if predictions made from them are not borne out in fact.

This approach is really quite familiar to you as a person in a Western culture. Consider the following. At some time or another you have probably been told by a finger-snapping friend that he is snapping his fingers to keep the elephants away. When you say "There aren't any elephants around here," he says "It works, doesn't it?" You, of course, dismissed this out of hand. Why?

Asked seriously to explain your position you would probably use arguments like the following: One, you would ask why on earth elephants would avoid finger snapping persons. It is not impossible that they do, but given all of the other reasons why they (the elephants) might not be in Cincinnati or Omaha, you think some explanation is in order. Also you are thinking that there are a lot of other things which should be true if the finger snapping person accurately understands his situation. For instance, elephants should be stampeding those persons who are not snapping their fingers. If you get an explanation which is that elephants have a delicate hearing system which is particularly sensitive to finger snapping, you would probably not dismiss your friend's idea so quickly. You can imagine ways this might be demonstrated to you to be true. Still, you would ask, given all those other plausible reasons why elephants are not stampeding present company: Is this the best explanation for the problem at hand?

If you thought these thoughts, you were thinking scientifically. You were asking for explanation (theory) and demonstration (empirical data). You were considering rival explanations and comparing them to this one. It remains only to raise questions like these in a systematic fashion. The research cycle provides the framework. The following diagram provides a rough sketch of the entire process. As we discuss its various aspects throughout the book you may want to refer to this diagram.

AN EXAMPLE OF THE RESEARCH CYCLE

In order to discuss the cyclical process, we must imagine a beginning point. Let us imagine that the beginning is observation of events. Further, let's imagine that the observations are direct observations of behavior and that the observer does not have relevant information other than his own observations. The frame of reference which causes the observer to see these particular events and not others may be conscious or

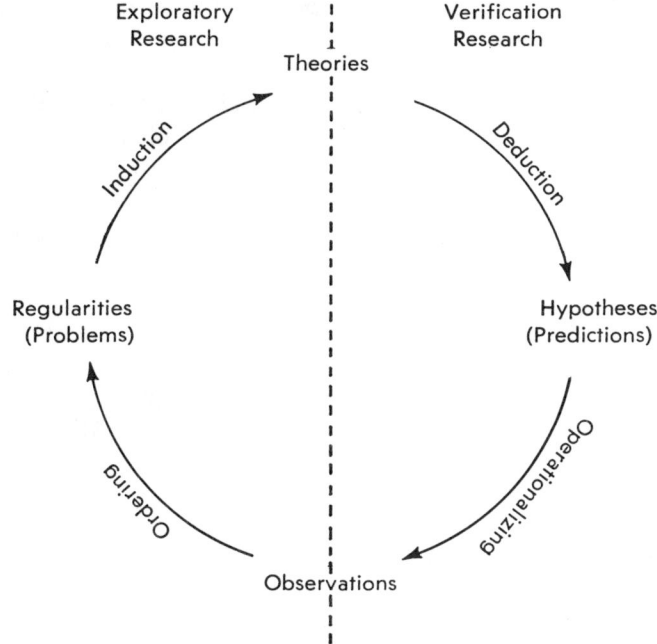

unconscious, scientifically motivated or not (remember all the different ways mapmakers see the fact of the earth).

Our imaginary observer sees behavior which he goes on to characterize as evidencing heroin addiction. This category 'heroin addicted' is more abstract than the behavior the observer actually saw—he saw individual people moving about, making noises and using their bodies in certain observable ways. He is interested, however, only in certain aspects of their behavior, aspects which he observes this group of people to have in common and which he has identified as heroin addicted behavior. The observer has summarized the behavior of a number of different individuals into a single category. In doing so, he has had to leave a great deal out; it no longer matters to him that the people were named Jack or Joe or Harry or that they were all tall or that a great many things about them were different. With respect to heroin addiction, they are the same. The behavior which interests him is now conceptually summarized.

He is interested in doing more than this, however. He would like to explain heroin addiction. He looks around for regularities which might provide him with clues to the puzzle. He discovers upon talking with his group of addicts that each of them was previously a marijuana user. The observer has uncovered a regularity, the explanation of which might be the explanation of heroin addiction he is seeking.

Our observer comes up with a very primitive theory. He speculates that human beings are experimenters, creatures who need to test the limits of human experience. Because it is in their nature to test what they can do, people who get started on minor drugs will progress to heavier and heavier drugs.

Why has the observer gone to the trouble of attempting a theoretical explanation? Why did he not stop at the point where he discovered the marijuana/heroin correlation, point out that these two things are connected and therefore predict that marijuana leads to heroin? There are several reasons. One is that extrapolation (predicting one event from its correlation with another) is no explanation. The person trying to *solve* a problem will not find this way of doing things (blind acceptance) very intellectually satisfying. In addition, there are practical reasons. Extrapolations are much more limited than theories and much less efficient. They are 'rules of thumb' or recipes: they don't give you very many choices or alternatives. Our observer is worried that unless he *understands* the regularity he has observed, he will spend a lot of time unnecessarily snapping his fingers or opposing marijuana. He therefore proposes a theoretical explanation for the observed regularity and subjects the explanation to a test.

The observer has identified a problem and imagined a plausible explanation. He has speculated that the relationship between marijuana and heroin can be explained by an aspect of human nature. This is a tentative explanation based on observation of a small number of cases. It might not be the only explanation of the correlation noted between marijuana and heroin but it is a reasonable explanation. It does what it is supposed to do. All that is required of a theory at this stage in the cycle is that it must be honest with respect to the observations at hand and it must place those observations in a larger explanatory context. It remains to a later phase of the research cycle to subject the explanation to a more rigorous test.

How do we go about testing a theory? First, we think about it logically. We ask if it is logically consistent and we decide, on a logical basis, what kinds of observable things ought to be true if the theory is. We predict that these things will be true and look to see if they are. It is good to make as many predictions as possible. In this hypothetical case, however, we will limit our predictions to the following two:

1) As drug use is one manifestation of a human need to test limits; all persons who use marijuana will progress to other more dangerous drugs.
2) As it is human nature to test the limits of experience, persons will manifest limit-testing behavior in their other behavior as well.

In social science these logical deductions are called "hypotheses." Notice that an hypothesis in social science is different from an hypothesis in mathematics.[2] In social science, hypotheses are tested and/or falsifiable predictions which are deduced logically from a theory. Hypotheses can be shown to be true or false. If they are true as predicted, this lends credence to the theory. Many hypotheses can be deduced from a single theory.

While it is in principle possible to show our hypotheses to be true or false, there remains the problem of how to do so. We must pay attention to problems of sampling and of measuring our concepts. We call this phase of research 'operationalization'. This refers to the process of relating our concepts to actual things, things that we can observe.

Sampling is the problem of deciding whom or what we want to observe. How can we be sure that the group of people we observe is typical, not different from the majority? If the group is exceptional when we thought it was typical we might think we had a theory about heroin addicts when in fact we had a theory about the type of heroin addict who is convicted or who volunteers for treatment or who lives in a particular neighborhood. Sampling strategies determine how far we can generalize our findings. A complete test would require us to sample everybody in the category of 'heroin addict'. This may not be easy. It is easier, for example, to sample voters than it is to sample people engaged in illegal activities, since it is easier to determine who is in the former group.

Measurement of concepts is a second problem in operationalizing hypotheses. There are no clear rules. A researcher must look at his concept and decide what kinds of observable things would indicate its presence. What evidence will you believe indicates a person falls into one or another drug use category? Will you take a person's word that he is or is not a drug user? Will you insist upon seeing the heroin injected? Do you want to be positive people inhale the marijuana before you will call them users?

---

[2]There is a reason in the history of words for both to be called hypotheses but it is usually more confusing to students than it is helpful. The same word is used because in each case the hypothesis states a relationship between two variables under given conditions (the conditions being the thesis or theory). In the research cycle however, the hypotheses emerge as a way of empirically testing the theory or thesis—something it does not do in mathematics.

Similarly, what kinds of activities should be examined for limit-testing behavior? The concept 'limit testing' must be translated. The observer must decide exactly what his concept means to him and subsequently what observable activity can serve to indicate it. Aside from drugs, how are limits tested? Do we want to look at war time behavior? The careers of race car drivers? The daily lives of housewives? How extreme will their behavior have to be before we will say they are testing limits? Must it be dangerous? Must the individuals show signs of psychological stress?

The things we have decided will indicate the concepts in our theory, are the things we look at. In deciding what to look at, the observer must cope with these problems and decide what observations will best relate to his concept and how much confidence he will place in the results. He then goes on to make the appropriate observations. In this case, imagine that we decide to interview marijuana smokers affiliated with a drug clinic, race car drivers who frequent a local drag strip, and Viet Nam combat veterans. We ask them questions regarding their behavior when they were confronted with an opportunity to engage in more dangerous behavior than that which they undertook initially. We ask if they know of marijuana users who have quit using drugs, or race car drivers who stopped racing, or combat soldiers who requested safer instead of more dangerous assignments. The responses to the questions are our new observations. These data should disprove our theory or support it.

What is observable, it should be remembered, may be directly or indirectly observable. We can observe behavior directly or, as is often the case, we 'observe' it indirectly. Much of what we do involves mediated observation. What we look at is behavior reported on a questionnaire, social characteristics reported in the census, grades obtained from the registrar. We may observe students in a reading class directly or we may 'observe' their grades in reading.

Notice that we have come completely around the research cycle and are once again making observations. The observations we are now making are informed by a scientific theory. Since this is true, these observations serve not only the function of providing us with puzzles (as before) but also the function of testing our theory.

At this point, we look at our interview results, our 'observations' to see whether or not in the lives of those we interviewed, one thing led to another in the way our theory predicted. We find that only a few marijuana users go on to heroin, many race car drivers lose interest in racing, and many soldiers retreat from combat. We must conclude our theory was wrong. These findings, however, are new problems. We know more than we did because we know some things are not true, and we have new puzzles. Maybe we found that, while people on the whole don't test limits in this way, young people seem to, or unmarried people or male people, or people sharing some other characteristic. What might explain *these* regularities? We proceed around the research cycle a second time, and on and on. In this way, theories are disproven, or modified to take account of new data.

If you are thinking that you might not have made some of the decisions we made, you are doing what you should be doing. If we wanted to know about all people, did we make a mistake in taking only people who were doing *obviously* dangerous things? Did we load our design in favor of getting only youthful respondents? Did we ask people the right questions? A score of other questions should be raised. No matter how authoritative a study may sound when written up, the author had to make the same kinds of decisions as we made here. It is the responsibility of all other social scientists, including students, to evaluate all these decisions and not to simply accept findings. It is from looking at all phases of research that we reach agreement about social realities or other problems we approach scientifically.

Because this is the case, you can see that it is very important for each researcher to tell in his reports exactly how he obtained in his findings. This includes a discussion of what issues, situations, conditions or observations suggested the problem initially, what theory is suggested to explain them, what the hypotheses are, how they were tested, and what the results were. Only if this information is included can others evaluate the study and contribute their ideas if they find fault. Most research, it should be emphasized, does not go all the way around the cycle but involves only some part of it. For example, an exploratory participant observation study may start with observations and end with a theory. A different researcher may then begin with the already proposed theory and test hypotheses deduced from it. Each researcher reports his own study.

As different theories are proceeding individually around the research cycle, they are also being compared to other theories. Let's imagine that some other observer has a theory that drugs are taken as a result of pressure from a person's peer group (his friends and associates). This observer feels that the desire to go along with the group is the most important motivation for taking drugs. Thus, an individual is apt to adopt the attitude toward drugs which is dominant in his group and behave accordingly. Specific hypotheses? If group members approve of heroin, an individual in that group will also approve; if group members approve of marijuana only, the individual will approve of marijuana only and avoid heroin. If group members disapprove of all drugs, the group member will disapprove of all drugs and avoid both marijuana and heroin.

Another theory might be that the most important reason for people becoming heroin addicts is external to themselves or their friends. We suppose here that people want only to smoke marijuana. Because they must buy marijuana, however, from illegal sources they become mixed up with drug pushers who try to hook them on addictive drugs so they will be more dependable customers. What hypotheses can be worked out here? Marijuana smokers will be more apt to become heroin users if marijuana is illegal than if it is legal? Heroin users will report that the person who suggested heroin to them was a person who wanted to sell it to them? What else?

These are only a few of the many possible theories which might explain heroin addiction. You have no doubt heard others. We are not attempting here to solve the problem of heroin addiction or present the literature on it. This example is presented only to show how theories are created and evaluated. For now, let's imagine that it is these suggested theories which are in competition. Predictions are made from each theory. If the particular theory is accurate these predictions indicate what types of people or in what kind of situations the greatest amount of heroin addiction should be found. We look for personality types, or we look at group attitudes, or we look at places where nonaddictive drugs are and are not legal. We look at the success of each theory and we compare results. Which theory predicts best? Perhaps all the theories predict somewhat but none well. This is often the situation in which the sociologist finds himself. He wants to eliminate, but it is difficult.

Looking at the indeterminateness of findings, researchers may do several things. They may feel present theories are not useful and start over, seeking an entirely different and original explanation. They may feel the theories need to be modified or combined in some way. These thoughts could lead to an altered and possibly improved theory. New predictions would be made and tested.

Researchers may also feel the test was inadequate and that one of the original theories needs better testing. We found that people did not test limits. Seemingly we should throw out the human nature theory. But someone suggests that the interview was not a good format or that our questions were not good, or our sample was biased. They propose that another test of this theory is necessary to eliminate it.

These problems plague all social research. Clear-cut findings are rare. Instead, social science goes forth slowly, depending usually on very small increments. People speculating about personal observations provide important fresh insights. People who combine theories or work out contradictions among them provide essential links to a growing knowledge. People who work on the problems of measuring concepts improve our chances of adequately testing a theory. The same people may not and probably will not carry out all phases of research. Yet the different phases are linked together as they all feed into the research cycle and into the ongoing effort of social scientists to improve our map of social reality.

The theories we have discussed stem from different guiding metaphors. Whenever a person asks "What explains this regularity?" assumptions and metaphors come into play —consciously or unconsciously. The first theory assumes the origins of behavior are to be sought in the immutable nature of man, in his basic unchanging needs. The second sees man as a cell in a social organism, a group. The organic whole controls individual cells and ejects foreign matter. The cells are similar and sympathetic. The third theory assumes that behavior results from more mechanical relationships, that it is controlled by the nature of the social machine. The organization of the different parts of the machine, as against their similarity or sympathy, determines their behavior.

These metaphors may seem very far removed from our concern with drug addiction. Our theorizing, however, relies on underlying metaphors like these, whether we are aware of it or not. If we think of man's nature as being fixed, we look to understand basic physiological or psychological needs and relate his social behavior to these needs. If we think man's nature is learned through his sympathetic participation in a group, we look at such things as norms and values and beliefs, socialization, conformity, and deviance. If we see behavior as structured by social organization, social machinery, we look at economic and political organization, at laws and bureaucracies, at job requirements and union rules.

Our small specific theories rely consciously or unconsciously on metaphors such as these. In turn, our theories test the metaphors. We test small specific theories which embody one or another set of assumptions. If many specific theories, however, seem to show that with respect to the particular problem behavior is psychological or normative or organizationally structured, the metaphor looks as though it might be an accurate map on a very grand scale. The specific theory is important in its own right, but this more general level of interpretation is important also.

This is the relationship between the 'grand theories' of sociology and the specific theories which are tested. This is a relationship which is not always easy to see or understand. When metaphors are worked out in detail, they are called "grand theories." The people who do this are the people who are usually called theorists. They include historic theorists like Durkheim and Weber and contemporary theorists like Robert Merton, Peter Blau, and Fred Cottrell.[3] Their theories do not enter directly into the research cycle. The research cycle processes specific theories, like those about heroin addiction. But these specific theories embody assumptions more or less congruent with grand theories. Hence results are seen as supporting or not supporting the grand theories as well as the specific theory.

If you think explicitly about guiding metaphors you may decide it is arbitrary to adopt one as a framework and reject others, especially since different frameworks are more or less useful in examining different problems. One student, after struggling through a number of abstract theories, threw up her hands stating "It seems to me there is a little bit of truth in everything." In the long run, however, it is our job to evaluate metaphors, determine which are the most important, how they fit together and complement one another, and when one or another is appropriate. We may find, for example, that values and job requirements both influence behavior. Yet at some point we ask also whether values grow out of the daily business of earning a living (economic organization), as Marx said, or whether people create economic patterns to be congruent with their beliefs, as Weber said.

Our more practical example may illustrate why we struggle with such problems. While social science is not explicitly concerned with social policy, the policy implications of whatever version of reality is accepted can easily be seen. The specific theories suggested here have very different implications. If we believed that because of the human personality marijuana leads naturally to dangerous drugs, and we think heroin is bad, we would likely outlaw marijuana, as we have. If we believed use of heroin is a matter of group opinion we would not worry about marijuana laws but would seek to educate people to the dangers of heroin. If we believed heroin use is increased by laws which make marijuana

---

[3]The grand theories of sociology include such ideas as: social behavior stems from belief systems (social action theory) from economic arrangements (materialism), from social exchanges (exchange theory) and from symbolic interaction (symbolic interactionism). This is a suggestive, not an exhaustive list. See further, Walter Wallace, *Sociological Theory* (Chicago: Aldine, 1969). This author attempts to delineate the major metaphors in contemporary sociology.

UNDERSTANDING SOCIOLOGY
The Research Cycle

illegal we would quickly legalize marijuana. Courses of action may be contradictory or we may simply lack the resources to do everything which seems desirable. Accepted versions of truth have real consequences. The research cycle is the social scientist's way of bringing his version as close to reality as possible.

SOME TERMINOLOGICAL DISTINCTIONS

There are a number of terminological differences which tend to unnecessarily confuse students. You may run into all of the following differences and perhaps more.

Terminological differences grow out of historical usage, day to day misusage, and various types of legitimate distinctions. We will mention a few examples. At some time or another you may hear the word 'hypothesis' refer to all of the things we have called 'regularity,' 'theory' and 'hypothesis.' This may relate to the fact that all of these are 'hypothetical.' In common usage people often speak of having an 'hypothesis,' when we would say they are proposing an ex-

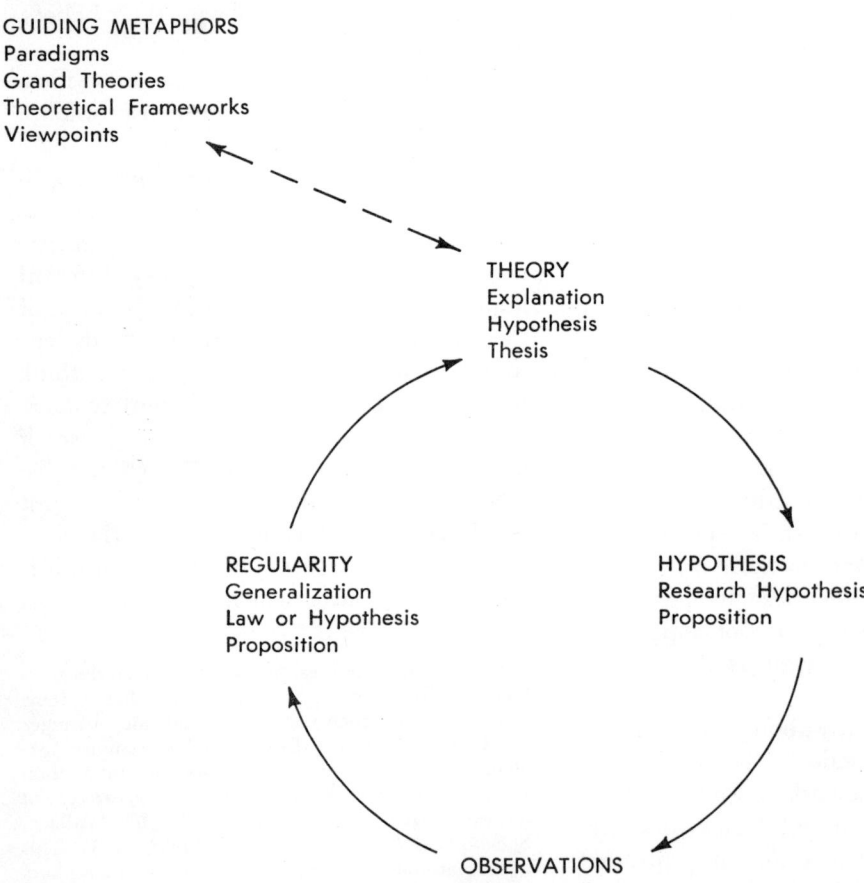

planatory 'theory.' These are casual differences.

Sometimes people do intend distinctions. For example, some people like to call an observed 'regularity' either a 'law' or an 'hypothesis.' They use the word 'law' when the regularity is supported by a huge amount of data and therefore seems to be very well established. They use the word 'hypothesis' to indicate a regularity which is more tentative or hypothetical. You might, for example, look around the sociology classroom and 'hypothesize' that more girls than boys take sociology. This regularity does not have the same weight of evidence as does the regularity which states that American women live longer than American men. If you want to make this distinction you might adopt this terminology which calls the former 'hypothesis' and the latter 'law.'

You should not, however, let terminological problems confuse you. In the future you might become interested in the history of science or in making further distinctions. You do not need to do these things to gain an understanding of the research process. For whatever reasons people use different words, it is clear to anyone who understands the research cycle what they mean by them. It should not confuse you or make the process seem unnecessarily complicated if people label these concepts somewhat differently.

For Further Reading

Wallace, Walter L. *The Logic of Science in Sociology*. Chicago: Aldine Press, 1971.
    This is a clear, concise analysis of the conceptual structure of sociology as a science. It is particularly useful in its incorporation of the literature about social science.

Lazarsfeld, Paul F. and Rosenberg, Morris. *The Language of Social Research*. New York: The Free Press, 1955.
    This volume is a reader including work by many sociologists on such subjects as: concepts and indices, multivariate analysis, the analysis of change through time, formal aspects of research on human groups, the empirical analysis of action, and general problems in the philosophy of social science. The student will get a good overview of the field, as well as more grounding in general sociology, from reading this.

3 | Designing Research

THE value of social science research is in its ability to move us closer to the explanation of a given problem. All of our activities are governed by this effort. No research is better because it uses a particular research method—unless that method is particularly appropriate to solving the problem. Suppose you are going to do research. You have thought of two problems which interest you. On the one hand you are interested in attitudes of college students toward different types of classes. You believe that some types are more effective. On the other hand you are interested in the organizational role of the mayor. You believe he fits into a network of relationships which influence his behavior and you would like to know what these are. What strategy should you adopt in studying these two problems?

You consider research strategy. You could reach quite a number of people if you would hand out a questionnaire which the respondents could fill out on their own. Is this appropriate? As you think about it, it occurs to you that you know a great deal about the daily lives of college students and next to nothing about the daily life of the mayor. Moreover, when you go to the library, you discover that other people have studied college students' responses to classes more often than they have studied mayors' networks of association. What might you ask on your questionnaire? You could probably put together a sensible questionnaire regarding college courses. On the basis of your experiences as a student, you could ask things like "Did you find this class: exciting, very Interesting, interesting, or boring?" "Did you recommend this class to others? yes no." "Did you discuss the material covered in this course outside of class? often, occasionally, rarely, never." You would not ask if a person considered it an honor to be class altarboy or whether students interact often with the foreman. You would not make the mistake of considering monthly attendance to be good, or forget to ask about the teacher. But the reason you would not make these errors is that you know quite a lot about universities.

Consider the case of the mayor. Your confidence that your questions would be sensible and relevant goes down. You can find out what the formal structure of city government looks like, but sociologists know that informal structure is equally important. With whom in the community does the mayor work? Whom should you ask about? How likely is it you will ask unimportant things and miss those which are important? Could you ask questions which could be answered *yes* or *no, frequently* or *never*? You probably don't know enough. If you ask whether he considered the newspaper more important than the Chamber of Commerce, would you feel confident you knew what *important* meant from his point of view? Under these circumstances it is not appropriate to use a questionnaire; that is, you would do better to consider doing an observational study rather than an interview study. If you chose observation, you would visit a mayor's office and observe what sort of things he did during his day, whom he saw and what sort of things concerned him. If you undertook an interview study, you would arrange a personal interview with some mayors. During the interview you would ask a small number of questions and encourage them to talk freely in the hope of learning relevant things you didn't know enough to ask. If you decided to interview rather than observe you would learn less about the individual case but you could reach more people.

Many other things enter into choosing a design for a research project. These include such considerations as whether you are one researcher or part of a group (some things are hard to do alone; some are done better this way), and what kinds of things you like to do or feel comfortable doing. But most important is that a social researcher keep his goal in mind. He wants to obtain reliable and interpretable data which will move his knowledge forward from where it is.

William Foote Whyte has provided us with a charming account of his efforts to locate an appropriate methodology for his now classic study of an Italian slum neighborhood.[1] He wanted to study the social structure of this slum, but neither he nor anybody else he knew could tell him much about it. Having chosen the neighborhood to study because it "best fitted my picture of what a slum district should look like," he nonetheless imagined some sort of a ten-man survey. He gradually scaled this down to a one or two-man door to door survey, but discovered he was quite uncomfortable with even this approach. He, a graduate student at Harvard, had a background and education which poorly suited him for asking useful questions.

He finally decided that simple, direct observation of people in the neighborhood would be the best strategy for learning something. Even in undertaking this his assumptions proved a handicap. He went to the Settlement House, an institution which provides a link between upper middle class persons and slum dwellers. This worked out all right, for it was through someone he met at the Settlement House that he gained entré. He notes in retrospect, however, that it would have made much more sense to make an initial contact through a local priest or politician. But this is something he learned only by doing his study (in which he discovered, among other things, that the Church and the local politics were important aspects of life in "Cornerville" and the Settlement House was unimportant.) There is nothing wrong with not knowing what you will find in your study before you do it. There would be something wrong with a ten-man survey of

[1] Wm. Foote Whyte, *Street Corner Society* (Chicago: The University of Chicago Press, 1955).

'Cornerville' which fit data into the stereotypes of Harvard students. Hence Whyte's decision to make friends and participate in the life of Cornerville was appropriate to the problem and proved much more valuable to other social scientists than the survey would have. Whyte's book provides rich material from which a sensible questionnaire might be put together. Not only would a subsequent questionnaire be in the appropriate language and ask about familiar things, it could build on the considerable theoretical insights of Whyte's study.

"SOFT DATA" AND "HARD DATA"

In evaluating research or in undertaking their own research, students are often trapped by their belief that certain types of studies are automatically more scientific and therefore better (or worse) than those which are done in other ways. Sometimes it is presumed that studies which use quantitative data are more scientific than those which do not use numerical data and are called qualitative. This attitude is reflected in the common use of the term "soft" for qualitative research and "hard" for the quantitative studies.

Implicit in this attitude is the further notion that a very large number of cases are necessary to a good study. Students often suggest, for example, that they are interested in studying some aspect of their home community but that it is probably too limited a project and is therefore not worthwhile or legitimate. This indicates a basic misunderstanding of social science. Whyte's account of his process of research is useful because it tells what the actual research process is like. In solving problems, strategies and methodologies are selected, cre-ated, and adapted. The criteria are how helpful a strategy seems to be in moving social science forward. Numerical measurement is appropriate only when the data can be meaningfully measured by numbers.

In a larger work on the subject of social scientific inquiry, one author has likened faith in methodological approaches to "Cargo Cults."

After the end of World War II there arose among the "primitive societies" of the South Pacific a phenomenon called 'cargo cults'. These were quasi-religious efforts to recapture the wealth and foreign delicacies that had been theirs as a result of occupation by armies of the "advanced" societies. The cargo cults constructed, albeit with primitive materials and designs, facsimiles of the docks and landing strips where the laden ships and planes had arrived. It was held as a matter of faith that, once their homes were created, the cargo bearers would appear.[2]

In short, a particular strategy may have no utility for a given problem.

Any given research method or strategy is exactly as good as its ability to help the given researcher solve his particular problem. A good study is one which is honest, accountable, and *responsible to science*. All of social life is interesting to sociologists, and science is the result of what is subjected to the research cycle.

EXPLORATION AND VERIFICATION

Where a given piece of research fits into the research cycle is important to its character and therefore to the way it should be evaluated. Exploratory research involves the creation of theories. Verification research attempts to falsify or confirm theories. Ex-

[2]Scott Greer, *The Logic of Social Inquiry* (Chicago: Aldine Press, 1969), p. 238.

ploratory research is inductive: general concepts and theories are proposed to explain specific observations. Verification research is deductive: specific observations are proposed as indicating general principles. Exploratory research produces theories which purport to be capable of generalization and of application to other situations. Verification research looks to see whether they are.

Because the categories came after the observations, the exploratory research which generated a theory may have been influenced by specific, unknown or unusual factors such as time, history, or geography. Movement from the general to the specific is a check on such errors. For example, William Foote Whyte indicated that the institutions which developed in the Italian community he studied were related to both the poverty and the exclusion of Italian-Americans from opportunities in the dominant society. His specific observations led him to speak about 'poverty' and 'exclusion.' Yet 'poverty' and 'exclusion' are terms which apply in other situations as well. If these are *general* principles we are working with it should not matter in what city his study was made: similar patterns should obtain wherever minority communities are excluded from opportunities.

In verification, we work to control the effects of idiosyncratic factors which may have biased the formulation of the original theory. We do this by determining whether the theory will work under other circumstances theoretically similar to but otherwise different from those which gave rise to it. The ideal way to do this, since we don't know what all the influences might be, is the random sample. Often however, this is impossible. We then think of the kinds of elements or factors which might have been important and take account of these. As we noted (Chapter I) Max Weber calls this process employing "mental experiments." We might in verifying Whyte's ideas be sure we included different cities in our study and different ethnic groups, since these seem to be the most likely biasing factors. Similarly, a theory about cities, developed in Chicago, should predict events in Los Angeles—a city which is different from Chicago in many respects.

Take another example. If complementary personality needs bring people together as mates as Freud suggested after observing patients in 19th century Germany, present day newlyweds at Northwestern University should display these complementarities also.[3] Those theories which continue to hold up under wide-ranging demands, we put our faith in. Those which do not we abandon or modify to take account of the failures.

When we require a theory to work in new situations we are opening it to falsification. If black minorities behave like earlier Italian minorities (in the specific ways predicted by the theory) we gain faith in the theory. If dominant males marry submissive females in an American university, Freud's theory looks plausible. If men land successfully on the moon, we trust the reports of physics which told us they would. But each of these predictions is potentially falsifiable. (They might land on Mars or not take off at all.) Interested observers can check the theory against reality and see *either* that the prediction holds or that it does not. If Freud's psychological theory does not accurately predict mate selection in different cultures

[3]Robert F. Winch, *Mate Selection* (Dubuque, Iowa: Wm. C. Brown Reprints, 1971).

as well as his own, we must conclude the theory is wrong. We might propose that his observations were better explained by German culture or Victorian marriage.

Ironically, the more you believe your theory is a good one, the more you should try to disprove it. Students who have been told for years to 'support' their ideas are usually surprised to learn that in social science (as in science generally) they must try to disprove them, testing them as rigorously as possible. Because of the curious nature of social scientific knowledge, one 'supports' his ideas by showing that he is unable to disprove or eliminate them as potential truths. We ask more and more of a good theory to see how good it is "stacking" the cards against it and risking each time that it may fall down or predict less well than another theory, and thereby be eliminated. All interested scientists will try to eliminate theories in the collective effort to locate the most powerful or best theories. We cannot be sure that a given theory is the best possible theory, anymore than we can be sure that a runner in a particular race is the best runner who might have come along; but the more races he enters and wins, the greater our confidence may be.

The strategy of empirically eliminating theoretical leads is a central norm in both exploratory and verificatory research. Collective falsification by the community of social scientists requires the application of two basic norms of science: 1) that each scientist considers his or her work falsifiable and frames it to this end and 2) that research processes and findings be made public.

Individually the social scientist is engaging in a similar process. At all points in the research cycle, scientists raise the question: How can I eliminate this proposition or theory? How can I prove myself wrong? Thus the participant observer is not simply standing around a given place, idly speculating about the people there. He is providing, within the limits of the study, the material (field notes which are as unbiased as possible) from which he may find exceptions to his interpretations of the situation he observes. His study, like all social science, relies on the rigorous use of empirical data as the means to falsify unjustified generalizations and theories. Rigor, within social science, is this adherence to the norms which allow for empirical falsification.

There are many different types of studies which fall into the categories 'exploration' research and 'verification' research. We will look in some detail at one example of each, in order to raise issues associated with the two phases of research, and to illustrate their general applicability as well as their difference. The particular strategies discussed should not be equated with exploration or verification more generally; there are many ways to explore and to verify. (We will look at a few others later.)

We have chosen to discuss 'participant observation' and 'experimental design' since these are usually regarded as very different strategies, the former appearing to be scarcely different from journalism (exploratory research, soft data) and the latter approaching the laboratory ideal of the physical sciences (verification research, hard data). However, notice in both the constant interaction between concepts and speculations, on the one hand, and empirical observations on the other. Also notice the common attention to proportions and exceptions to the rule. Finally, note that in both types of research, an investigator attempts to multiply check-points: 1) generating additional hypotheses (what else should logically be true?); 2) increasing methodological angles on the subject (what other types of observations should indicate the same patterns?). As you read the next chapter, you may find it useful to refer back to the graphic representation of the research cycle on page 15.

For Further Reading

Webb, Eugene J.; Campbell, Donald T.; Schwartz, Richard D.; and Seechrist, Lee, *Unobtrusive Measures: Nonreactive Research in the Social Sciences*. Chicago: Rand McNally and Company, 1966.

This is a shrewd and charming discussion of the ways social scientists can develop cross-checking measures of social reality. Its authors are from a wide range of disciplines and their combined knowledge is at once interesting and useful.

4 | Participant Observation and Experimental Design

PARTICIPANT observation is research in which the sociologist attaches himself personally to a group or institution in order to observe behavior at first hand. He builds a theory out of his personal observations. In some types of participant observation, the observer is looking for certain things (e.g., how workers respond to a female as against a male boss). In others his attention is very open and diffuse.

The participant observer may actually participate in the group or observe it only. Some people feel there is a terminological difficulty here, and speak of participating and nonparticipating observers. Others call both forms participant observation, but refer to participant observers as being either 'passive' or 'active', depending on whether the individual tried to keep his participation at a minimum or joined actively into group life. This latter group feels total nonparticipation is rare or impossible.[1] Observation which is directed to specific things may be used in tests of theories; but we will be interested here in the type of exploratory observation where attention is diffuse.

The participant observer may spend a few weeks or several years with a group. A longer time period is generally assumed to provide a better basis for understanding. If the participant observer is not going to be with the group he studies full time, he tries to be with them at different times and on different occasions. A participant observer who was studying a grade school classroom would be sure his visits to the classroom were at various times of the day, and every school day during the week. An observer who visited a classroom Friday afternoons only would get the impression that school rooms were much less orderly than one who visited on Tuesday mornings.

The participant observer keeps extensive notes recounting what he has seen and heard. In observing and in writing up his notes, he pays close attention to detail. Because he is interested in generating new concepts and hypotheses (hypothetical generalizations), he wants to control the influence of the frame of reference he brings to the situation. He does not want to assume he knows beforehand what is impor-

[1] It is certainly very difficult for an observer who hangs around very long to remain entirely outside of the group. An example is the student studying a drug clinic who found himself the only person not doing anything when a rescue call came in.

tant, but rather to allow the importance to emerge. He cannot do this completely, but he does have some rules which help him to minimize the effect of his preconceptions, his "conceptual blindfolders," and to see things in a genuinely new light.

He achieves this by observing and recording what he sees in the lowest possible unit of abstraction. He tries to avoid summarizing his observations in terms of categories which reflect his prior frame of reference. For example, he would avoid saying that he observed several 'poor' people enter the room. "Poor" is not something to be observed. He observed something else, the way these people were dressed or what they said about themselves. These observations are what should be reported. He wants observations which will be usable data in spite of the fact his perspective changes—and it will as he learns more.

His data must be such that he or somebody else in the community of scientists can look at it, evaluate, and reinterpret it. Using the example of clothing and its interpretation, imagine you arrived at a college campus in the mid-sixties to do a study of student life. You write in your notes that a group of very poor students behave in a quite rebellious fashion. Your early idea is that class warfare is on the rise, with the poor students revolting against the richer ones. This is plausible except later you learn that students who call themselves 'hippies' dress in a manner which is in some ways similar to that of very poor people (in spite of the fact that they are usually well off). You now formulate a theory about hippies. You would like to be able to go back to your notes and check your ideas on hippies against *all* the behavior you have observed, but you can't know when the person you described was a hippie doing something and when it was someone else, because your notes don't tell you what you meant by 'poor' at that time. Interpretations and conclusions would be different if you said that the person picketing reported he was unable to pay his tuition than if you said the person picketing had long hair, patched jeans, army surplus shoes, and beads. A similar problem might have arisen in the hypothetical study of drug addiction if heroin withdrawal symptoms had been labelled as epileptic fits.

The effort to see things in a fresh way also means that the participant observer takes notes on what seem at the time to be irrelevant things. But he is trying not to determine relevance too early. For example, it is better to include verbatim conversations than to assume you know the entire meaning of a conversation between two people.

Here are two good examples of participant observation notes. One is taken from a study of a French Canadian Community done by an eminent sociologist. The other set is from a study of a mental hospital done by an undergraduate.

The newspaper is full of the plans for tomorrow's celebration and for the bonfire (Feu de St. Jean) to be lighted in the Academy grounds this evening. We saw the English school principal and his wife today. They knew nothing of the plans for the celebration. According to him, St. Jean-Baptiste means nothing to the English except that they have to be careful to lay in a supply of groceries the day before, because the stores are to be closed.
At 8:00 P.M. the benches in the park were full —of women and children, which is unusual— and gradually the streets filled with people, also mostly children. About 8:30 the school boys' band marched around the square and took up a position in front of the presbytery.

UNDERSTANDING SOCIOLOGY
Participant Observation and Experimental Design

A car then drove up near by, and from it emerged two city aldermen, who proceeded to distribute flags to the children. The flags were of blue, with a white cross in the center and a white fleur-de-lis in each corner. The children had been lined up, without much order, to receive the flags and to march to the Academy grounds. The smiling aldermen, besieged by reaching hands, gave out the flags with a magnanimous air. The cure and a couple of city officials stood on the porch of the presbytery to receive the homage of the children. Before the last of the flags were given away, the band played and marched away, followed by several hundred children with flags more or less intact.[2]

July 14, 1972

The floor staff follows a very set procedure for taking patients over to the cafeteria during mealtime. It is a proceeding that is strictly followed for all meals. Two staff members—one male, one female—take the patients off the ward (one in front, one in back of the group). The patients go in single file over to the cafeteria, which is outside the building and directly across the street. When they get to the cafeteria the first staff member unlocks the door and lets the patients in until all are in, then the last staff member locks the door. The patients have lunch in normal cafeteria style, while the staff members watch over the patients. When everyone is finished (the staff will hurry those patients who are slow eaters), the staff brings the patients back, following the same procedure. This cafeteria, one of several on the hospital grounds, services only Kent House. Lunch is from 11:00 to 1:00, with one-half of the wards going from 11:00 to 12:00 and the other half from 12:00 to 1:00. If a patient tries to escape while going over to or returning from the cafeteria, the male aide is in charge of going after the patient. The female aide, after the patients are secured, will notify the supervisor's office, who will dispatch the hospital security force.

Today a patient who was very hyperactive in an irritable way collapsed and hit her head on a chair. Even though she was uninjured, the staff was required to fill out an incident report. The report records the time, description of the incident, place, and whatever injuries. The doctor is also notified.[3]

After accumulating a large number of notes, the participant observer adopts a strategy called 'analytic induction.' He sets about describing what he saw in more general terms. He is careful that descriptive statements are true to his observations. He checks and double checks his generalization against his data. Having made a statement which seems to be true, he goes back to his notes, looks for all the instances which seem related to the generalization and checks to see if what he says occurs in such instances occurred in this instance. He does not want to describe as typical events which were really not typical. It is easy to overemphasize things which are striking or memorable or in keeping with a prior viewpoint. The participant observer seeks to avoid these pitfalls through careful reference back to his notes. This is his check against erroneously saying heroin users were observed to be former marijuana users if, in fact, this were only true half of the time. The research procedure differentiates the research of a participant observer from the knowledge that any observant person comes to have about groups in which he is a participant. The latter does not keep notes for the purpose of locating errors in his analysis.

An example of this process can be taken from the study mentioned above, Everett Hughes's study in French Canada. Hughes' impression was that there was little social

---

[2]Everett Hughes, *French Canada in Transition* (Chicago: The University of Chicago Press, 1963), p. 149.

[3]Cameron W. Clark, Private field notes. Collected in connection with a senior thesis, *The Social Control Systems of a State Mental Hospital*. Lake Forest College, 1973.

intermingling between the French and the English Canadians. Hypothesizing this as a regularity, he would go back to his notes and look for all observations bearing on this point. The first statement in the quoted notes would be one such instance; it involves a major French social event and the response of one English couple. He looks further at his accounts of French/English funeral attendance since funerals seem to fit the category (social). He also looks to see if he has recorded any dating between French and English young people. He looks for all references to things which fall under the category he has described.

In writing this up, Hughes tells the reader at some length who was in attendance at various funerals for the purpose of indicating that English persons did not attend French funerals. But he also tells you about any 'negative cases'—cases where his generalization did not hold. These stand to falsify his generalizations unless he can account for them theoretically, or persuade you they are so infrequent as to not really contradict his generalization. Having brought forth a large amount of evidence confirming the French-English social separation, Hughes reports the following exceptions and tries to account for them.

An unmarried daughter of a French "first family" came to a small tea at the house of a high industrial executive; it was a tea held after tennis matches in which she had played on the company team. Another French girl of similar standing often turned up informally at an English house which is the rendezvous from which some of the unmarried English men of the minor executive class start off on swimming parties and canoeing and skiing expeditions. An English couple once went to this girl's house for cocktails before a dance. Another French girl was there with a young American college man who was playing on the town baseball team for the summer. A total of perhaps four girls of this type have some social life with English people. They are charming, accomplished girls of the best social connections but of such an age that their prospects of marriage dwindle each day. The town contains no unmarried French Canadians of the age, social standing, and prospects to be suitable mates for them.[4]

A paragraph such as this often slows down the narrative, but it is a sign of responsible attention to empirical data and to the community of researchers who want to know what Hughes means by his broader statements and how much confidence should be placed in his analysis.

Howard S. Becker describes the systematic way a participant observer handles the disparate kinds of data gathered in field observation. In the following quote, he is talking about a study he and several colleagues did in a medical school in Kansas:

Suppose, for example, that the observer concludes that medical students share the perspective that their school should provide them with the clinical experience and the practice in techniques necessary for a general practitioner. His confidence in the conclusion would vary according to the nature of the evidence, which might take any of the following forms: 1) *Every* member of the group said, *in response to a direct question,* that this was the way he looked at the matter. 2) *Every* member of the group *volunteered* to an observer that this was how he viewed the matter. 3) *Some given proportion* of the group's members either *answered* a direct question or *volunteered* the information that he shared this perspective, but none of the others were asked or volunteered information on the subject. 4) Every member of the group was asked or volunteered information, but *some given proportion said* they viewed the matter from the differing perspec-

[4]Everett Hughes, *French Canada in Transition*, (Chicago: University of Chicago Press, 1963), p. 166.

tive of a prospective specialist. 5) No one was asked questions or volunteered information on the subject, but *all members were observed to engage in behavior* or to make other statements from which the analyst *inferred* that the general practitioner perspective was being used by them as a basic, though unstated, premise. For example, all students might have been observed to complain that the University Hospital received too many cases of rare diseases that general practitioners rarely see. 6) *Some given proportion* of the group *was observed* using the general practitioner perspective as a basic premise in their activities, but *the rest of the group* was not observed engaging in such activities. 7) *Some proportion* of the group *was observed* engaged in activities implying the general practitioner perspective while *the remainder* of the group was observed engaged in activities implying the perspective of the prospective specialist.[5]

Proportions inform the logical process through which a theory is formulated, tying the theory directly and continuously to empirical observations. Suppose that Hughes in checking his notes had found that there was a clear French-English social separation in only half of the total social occasions he had recorded. He would see that his generalization was untrue (perhaps he had been overly impressed by certain kinds of events at the expense of others). The next step would be another attempt to formulate a descriptive regularity. If, on the other hand, he had found (as he did) that there were only a few instances which diverged from the regularity, he would look to determine whether some additional factor explained why these particular cases differed from the others. If necessary, he would modify the generalization to take account of these cases.

The instances which do not fit the overall regularity are called "negative cases" or "deviant cases." Close examination of them and modification of a generalization to take account of them is the core of the "analytic induction process." A researcher must come up with reasons why these cases do not falsify his proposition, or he must modify the proposition to take account of them.

These descriptive regularities are not the end of exploratory research. Some explanation which logically relates the various observed regularities must be proposed. Hughes goes on to propose a theory of urbanization to explain his observations. This attempt at theoretical explanation is a second important difference between the participant observer and the informed group member. The latter has learned to get along day to day but his perspective is what we have earlier called 'practical vision.'

Research is improved by supplementing one methodology with a complementary one. A good social researcher is an opportunist. If data collected by various methods differ in the pictures they present, this is something which should be considered. If other types of data concur with that collected in the main line of inquiry, the researcher is encouraged. There are important methodological reasons to supplement one data-gathering strategy with others, since each has its biases and pitfalls. It is also intuitively reasonable. A person solving a problem looks for help wherever he can find it. He seizes any relevant documents (such as published reports, letters, or newspaper articles) and compares these with his observations. He asks questions. If he finds knowledgeable informants, he so-

[5]Howard S. Becker, "Problems of Inference and Proof in Participant Observation" in George McCall and J. L. Simmons (eds.) *Issues in Participant Observation* (Reading, Mass: Addison-Wesley Publishing Co., 1969), p. 252.

licits their help and welcomes any insights and tips they may provide. One of the authors of this book, for example, carried out a participant observation study in the office of a city mayor. The mayor was a keen and self-conscious observer whose insights were invaluable.[6] If group members know there is a study under way, they are apt to offer tips such as "There's something going on tomorrow I think you'd be interested in."

Additional data is all advantageous—both that which comes in casually and that which the observer collects purposively (as through interviewing). We multiply data-gathering technics to uncover errors in our theories. If formal statments which people make in interviews do not accord (are not consistent) with remarks that they make in everyday conversation, this is a problem to be dealt with. If two informants differ in their interpretations of a situation, this is a situation which the observer should try to reconcile within his theory. Unless the participant observer can account theoretically for discrepancies he uncovers, he has cause for concern that his theory is not adequate. Whether he is forming or testing a theory, a person doing research is always looking for facts or phenomena which contradict his propositions. Different data sources are often sources of apparent contradiction and therefore a resource in theory-building.

A proposed theory based on exploratory research procedures remains to be tested or verified. The process has involved movement from specific observations to a suggested set of theoretical relations which refer to more general categories. The determination of the validity of these general relationships is the job of verification research.

EXPERIMENTAL DESIGN

Attaching meaningful concepts to raw data and measuring concepts with raw data (observations) requires imaginative leaps between the concrete observation and the abstract concept. The interpretive problem involved in testing a theory is the reverse side of the one we encountered when we were creating concepts to describe observations, and theories to explain them. Now we must think of (deduce) observable cases which are logically included in the abstract categories.

These cases may include but should not be limited to those which inspired the theory if we are to learn whether the more abstract relations hold. In an earlier chapter, we presented a theory that heroin addiction was one manifestation of a human characteristic: limit testing. We do not want to conclude, however, should we find that marijuana users go on to heroin, that this alone verifies our theory about limit testing. Hence we try to think of other opportunities for limit-testing, where, logically the same behavior should be observable. Only if our theory holds up in all of its logical forms, can it be assumed a legitimate explanation for even the original observations. This is the problem of verification: moving from the abstract category to particular observable instances. A person with a research problem will quickly appreciate the gap between the concrete and the abstract since it is his imagination which must connect the two. He will also appreciate the importance of judgment and discretion in research.

[6] Ann Lennarson Greer, *The Mayor's Mandate: Municipal Statecraft and Political Trust* (Cambridge, Mass.: Schenkman Publishing Co., 1974).

UNDERSTANDING SOCIOLOGY
Participant Observation and Experimental Design

A sociology class undertook to evaluate the experimental seminar program at their school. The seminars were small, discussion-oriented, interdisciplinary and geared to topics of current interest. These had been instituted to provide an alternative to larger, lecture-based disciplinary survey courses. The theory (or more accurately, theories) behind the various aspects of the seminar program had not been worked out to any great extent by the sponsors of the program. Nevertheless, the program was the outgrowth of certain assumptions and theories of education, and thereby provided a test of those theories. Generally speaking, the underlying theory was that serious learning and commitment to education arise in situations where students can become involved personally (in small groups) with topics of immediate interest to them. This was presumed to be in contradistinction to disciplinary courses where relevance to life problems is not immediately apparent and student participation is relatively detached. Thus courses such as "The Many Dimensions of Poverty" were offered as alternatives to courses which surveyed the topics and methods used in fields such as sociology or economics.

The sociology class charged with the evaluation sought to discover: Did the seminars have the desired effect? The first thing which occurred to class members was to ask the freshmen in the seminars how they felt about the seminars. Almost as quickly, it occurred to somebody that they wouldn't know how this compared to the other courses unless they also asked students from the other courses about their classes. It was decided to talk to students from both groups (the students in seminars and a control group of students from other classes).

In fact, the seminar program could be seen as similar to a classical experiment. One group of students received the 'treatment' (the seminars); one group did not. If the theory behind the educational experiment was correct, the two groups should differ in predictable ways. These predictions are the hypotheses of the experiment. Hypotheses predicted that seminar students would find their classes more intellectually stimulating, and that they would be more positively influenced by them in their attitudes toward education.

OPERATIONALIZATION

What questions should be asked? Two kinds of data/information had to be determined: 1) Had the seminars actually had the characteristics (topicality, relevance, discussion) upon which the desired consequences were theoretically dependent? 2) Did the predicted outcomes occur? The presence or absence of these outcomes, given the necessary conditions, would confirm or falsify the theory.

What questions should be asked? Since we are interested in empirical data of the sort we can agree upon, the hypotheses had to be "operationalized" or translated from concepts into observable events. One of the hypotheses was that students would find the seminars more intellectually stimulating. Should we ask outright: "Did you find this course stimulating?" "If you had to answer that, what would you say?", one student asked. And another questioned: "Supposing they say 'yes' or 'no' or 'sort of,' what would it mean?" Does the concept mean whatever the respondent thinks it means? If so, the respondent is in effect defining the concept 'stimulating' for the sociologist. Another student suggested that this would not be so good since the class would not know what the respondents meant and whether each respondent meant the same thing. It would be better to ask about specific things that people do or don't do. What is the specific behavior the word 'stimulating' summarized in the first place? How do people who are 'stimulated' behave? What observable things do they do? Do they attend classes more regularly than otherwise? Do they talk about stimulating topics to their friends outside of class? Do they work harder? Each of these was a suggested indicator. If it seemed appropriate, a question was formed around it.

A second issue raised by the seminars was whether the smaller classes might not facillitate social adjustment to college. This is an additional theoretical problem but one which interested the student investigators. Do small classes with increased student interaction contribute to more rapid and effective adjustment to college? We bring this second problem up because the difficulty of operationalizing the concept is even more striking. "Are you socially adjusted?" demonstrates the problem of the direct conceptual question which we discussed as "Did you find this course stimulating?" Again, the students in the class decided that the freshmen would not be able to answer such a question, and any answers they did provide would be uninterpretable. What does the concept 'social adjustment' mean to the researchers? How do socially adjusted people differ from those who are not? Can a class experience be considered to have contributed positively to social adjustment if the students know each other's name? if they have made friends in class? There are no rules for determining observable measures other than conventions and judgment. It is difficult to feel completely satisfied with any indicator (measure), but all scientific knowledge is based on this indirect sort of evidence.

Donald T. Campbell has observed:

There are not intrinsically valid measures for anything. We only know indirectly. Analysis of any physicist's instrument such as the cloud chamber shows some residual products of the beta particle that went past it—it doesn't show the beta particle.[7]

Instrumentation

For each of the behaviors which are assumed to indicate the concept, potential answers are considered. Again, interpretability is the criterion for selection. When is a yes/no choice the best, that is, a simple indication that something did or did not happen, was or was not present? When do we want to know how much of something is present? We might ask: Do you know the names of your classmates? ___ yes ___ no. Or we might provide as choices ___ many, ___ some, ___ a few, ___ none, or we might ask for a specific number: How many? Or provide a list of groupings ___ over 20, ___ 15-19, ___ 11-14 and so on down to 0. We might ask students to name as many names as they can and count the number. Thinking over these choices, the researchers would decide whether "yes" and "no" gave them as much

[7] Donald T. Campbell, "Administrative Experimentation, Institutional Records and Non-Reactive Measures," in *Organizational Experiments, Laboratory and Field Research*, ed. Wm. N. Evan, (New York: Harper & Row, Publishers, 1971), p. 171.

of a notion of acquaintanceship as they need or whether they need more information to find out what they want to know. Are rough indications enough, or do they need the exact number? We call these decisions "instrumentation."

The response must provide for an adequate comparison between the control group and the experimental group. If regarding acquaintanceship we ask for a *yes* or *no* answer, it is likely the vast majority in each group would say *yes*, that they know some names. This measure then is too crude for this variable. (a variable is any trait, quality, or characteristic which can vary in magnitude in different individual cases). If the question was, "Are the issues and questions covered in this course ones that you would like to study again in another course?", a simple yes/no might be adequate. Would it really make sense to ask how many times you might like to do it again? Probably not.

As these examples indicate, the researcher anticipates possible answers to questions in the interest of posing good questions. The kind of problems which may nonetheless arise may be illustrated in the following questions which were proposed for use in the seminar study. One related to amount of work done. The other is a background variable (included to allow for a check on the possibility that intellectual commitment might be related to attributes of the students rather than attributes of the courses).

Look for the problems.

1) Have you used library or other reference materials?
   _____ in this course
   _____ in other courses
   _____ in this and other courses

2) Have you selected a major area of concentration?
   _____ yes
   _____ no
   If yes, what is it? _____

The first question does not provide a place for students to say that they did not use reference materials in any course. Another choice, "_____ in no course" should have been provided. Otherwise some people cannot answer honestly and some will feel pressure to answer dishonestly since their answer is not present. The question is not a good one.

The second sample question involves a phrase "major area of concentration" which confused some students. Of those who were asked to respond, some answered that they had selected a major area of concentration. Of these, some specified "English or "Sociology" (what had been intended) but others said their major area of concentration was "the Second World War" or the "Environment."

Problems of instrumentation can usually be avoided by a pretest of the questionnaire. This is where a preliminary version of the questionnaire is administered to a small number of people who are asked to indicate any confusion, irritation, or discomfort they found in answering. "Pretests" serve as trial runs where difficulties and confusions can be corrected before the questionnaire is administered to the large sample. If problems like these are not corrected, it is impossible to interpret the answers.

The researcher asks a number of different questions regarding each concept. He would never equate hard work and intellectual stimulation on a one to one basis.

Rather he would look at several behaviors, such as talking about the class to friends, attending often, and so forth. Since his measures are not perfect, he uses a number of them and looks for meaning in the patterns.

Statistical Analysis

In deciding who should respond to the questionnaire and in analyzing the responses, statistics may be needed. (The larger the number of cases, the more important this becomes.) Statistics tell you how many persons you will need to sample if you are to generalize to the whole group (how many freshmen are needed to get an accurate picture of the whole group). Usually the larger the sample the better, but in a carefully selected sample, a small number may provide very accurate information. George Gallup and Lou Harris ask only 1200 people about their voting preferences and predict the votes of seventy million people. The key idea of the random sample is that each person in the group (each voter, for example) has an equal chance of getting into the sample. The sample is not biased; it is representative. A shopping plaza poll is not statistically valid since it is biased in favor of shoppers—who may be disproportionately female, young or middle-aged, healthy and so forth. A random sample should get responses from all equally.

The kind of statistics normally used by social scientists in analyzing their data are statistics which compare the two or more groups studied and tell whether the differences between them are real differences or simply normal variation. We know that if we measure the heights of ten freshmen and obtain an average, it may be a different average than that which we get when we measure the heights of ten other freshmen. We expect the same kind of normal variation if we ask freshmen how hard they work, and average their responses. The question is whether the difference between the group averages is statistically so great that we assume something besides normal variation is at work. That is, if the difference is unusually large (statistically significant) we consider this an indication that something is causing the difference and we assume it is the factor which we have said would produce such a difference when we made the prediction. Therefore it confirms our theory.

Plausible Rival Explanations

We can't be sure, however, that our theory is thereby ultimately verified. As we know, many other theories might account for the findings. Some of these are known to us, some not. Validated predictions are encouraging confirmations of the proposed theory, but it is possible that they confirm not our theory but something else. What might it mean if seminar students are found to work harder than students in other courses? Does it mean the seminars inspired the harder work, or that better students prefer seminars? If seminar students are more friendly with their classmates than are students in control classes, does this mean the class situation produced this, or did more gregarious people choose the smaller classes? The social scientist must consider rival explanations and decide whether they are plausible enough to interfere with the clear interpretation of his findings. If the answer is 'yes', he should consider ways to clarify his conclusions. Even if he does not know of any such explanations, he must be cautious.

We may call such possibilities "threats to validity." There are two general types of threats: internal threats to validity and external threats to validity. Both types can be seen in this study. The first is present when something about the study makes it impossible to know whether the experimental conditions made a difference in the particular instance. Deciding that the seminars inspired harder work would be dubious if it was possible that actually the harder working students had enrolled in the seminars and the lazier students had taken the regular classes. Internal validity is whether what we say is true about a particular instance is really true.

External validity concerns the validity of generalizing and applying the findings to other situations. Our theories are supposed to be generalizable to other situations theoretically like ours. Problems can arise if something about the study makes generalizing invalid. For example, the students in the seminars might have behaved differently because the seminars were new and experimental. The conclusion that the seminar classes were more intellectually stimulating would be incorrect if the result only occurred under experimental and not normal conditions. We might have a theory about experimental groups masquerading as a theory about seminar students. Since there are many studies which show that experimental groups do enjoy the distinction of being involved in experiments and behave differently because of this, such considerations are very important. Another concern is that the test affects the responses, for example, if respondents answer what they thing the interviewer wants them to say.

This is not a council of despair. Researchers can develop methods for controlling problems like these. If uncontrolled, they may still be able to estimate the likelihood that the alternative explanation is the true explanation. The questionnaire might have included questions regarding how much time the student put into this and other courses to determine whether the seminar or control group were generally harder workers, and so forth. They can also find information and protection against known pitfalls (those that have turned up in previous studies).

The important point to remember is that when the social scientist looks at findings which he is asked to believe support a theory, he asks himself: "Is there any other explanation for these findings which has not been taken into account?" We have talked about the process of evaluating competing theories; threats to validity pose the same kind of challenge to a theory. They suggest that some other explanation seems as likely or more likely to have produced the findings you predicted than the theory you have proposed.

METHODS OF FALSIFICATION

Replication

We have seen that there are problems associated with translating the concepts in our hypotheses into observable events. Inevitably the observable events seem less than perfect indications of the concept. We have seen also that other factors such as the way we selected our sample or the desire of an interviewee to please the interviewer may have produced spurious conclusions. We know further that these known problems are only those which have so far been discovered. We know finally that theories we have not imagined may be more accurate than the one we have before us.

These are problems which can never be finally solved. They tell us why our theories must be forever tentative and why we continually seek new insights into falsification. Since there are many uncontrolled factors even under the best of circumstances, we adopt general as well as specific strategies of falsification. One is "replication."

If we repeat studies under theoretically similar but otherwise different circumstances, assumptions hidden in the first research may be uncovered. We may discover theoretical limitations we had not understood. We may discover rival explanations we had not considered. As an example of theoretical limitations, we may discover that our theory about freshman seminars applies only part of the time. We see perhaps that it holds for large but not small schools. By trying the theory out in other schools, this theoretical limitation comes to light. We can modify our theory to take account of this. (After which we test the modified theory.) A similar situation would exist if we found that our theory about social pressure and drug use held up for persons under but not over 30 years of age.

We may also uncover rival explanations through replication. We might find that our seminar results occur only where seminars have been instituted on an experimental basis and not where they are part of the established ongoing program. This alerts us to the possibility that the experimental situation may have produced the positive results, and not the seminar format. In this case, the theory seems to be wrong (it had appeared to be true but has now been falsified).

Replication, then, is a very important means of falsifying theories and of discovering their limitations. Social science has not been as rigorous in replicating studies as have the physical sciences. Of this fact Campbell makes the following observation:

... truths are buttressed by hundreds or thousands of replications. ... An essential part of the physical sciences is the bandwagon effect of problem popularity which either confirms or erases every promising lead. This is not to be confused with the bandwagon of fads ... in which everyone starts applying something on the blind faith that it has been proven elsewhere.[8]

In a piece directed to the possibility of classes of students conducting surveys in their local communities, Devine and Falk point out the need for replication also:

Social science may presently face the danger of being seduced by the false doctrine that bigger and bigger research, conducted by fewer and fewer organizations, will somehow result in better research. ... We judge that the coordination of research in different parts of the country, holds more promise than the centralization of research. This coordination could be accomplished in many ways. One way is the replication of survey questionnaires in many cities throughout the country, thereby allowing a comparison of the results and an assessment of contextual effects of a particular city or regional contexts in the obtained results.[9]

These two quotes again indicate that a replication study (and the falsification strat-

[8] Donald T. Campbell, "Administrative Experimentation, Institutional Records, and Non-Reactive Measures," p. 172.

[9] Richard P. Devine and Laurence L. Falk, "Social Surveys: A Research Strategy for Social Scientists and Students" (Morristown, N. J.: General Learning Corporation, 1972), p. 4.

egy generally) may seem to falsify a theory in its entirety or it may seem to falsify only parts of it. In the latter case modifications of the theory, taking account of "contextual effects" are proposed for subsequent tests.

Triangulation of Methods

Another general strategy by which we try to obviate the weaknesses in our ability to measure concepts, the biases and the reactive effects of our tests, and our inability to know all relevant factors is to look for other substantiating evidence. By triangulation is meant the gathering of different types of data, the coming at a problem in different ways, from different beginning points. This may mean supplementing interview data with observational data (e.g., asking for racial attitudes *and* observing social clustering of black and white persons). It may mean any combination of methods, including the common approaches we use and any others which may be useful. Ingenuity in finding relevant data and in seeing the relevance of available data is an asset to the 'experimenter' as it was to the participant observer. Campbell and his associates have proposed especially imaginative alternative data sources in their book, *Unobtrusive Measures*.[10] An example they suggest is measuring the popularity of a museum exhibit by checking on how often the floor tile in front of it has to be changed.

Any methodology has its biases and shortcomings. Triangulation takes advantage of the fact that these biases and shortcomings are different for the different methodologies. We shall consider the strengths and weaknesses of some of the most common methodological approaches in the next section. For purpose of example, we will simply note that interviews regarding preferred museum exhibits might produce data biased toward what the interviewed person thought was the proper answer. Alternatively, changes of tile might indicate that people shuffled their feet more in front of this exhibit, or that it was in the path leading to the rest room. Since these methods of gathering data have different problems, however, we can be much encouraged if they support the same hypothesis. One author has observed:

It is somewhat like the process of locating a forest fire from a distant smoke. If we have a map locating three fire-watchers relative to each other and the terrain, and if we ask each to locate the smoke from his point of view, we can draw three lines which will intersect and locate the fire on the map in one spot and one only. . . .[11]

Using a second type of method for examining an hypothesis is similar to the generating of multiple hypotheses, the use of multiple questions to get at a single concept, and the replication of studies in different contexts. Like each of these, the assumption behind triangulation is that a theory should hold up in spite of changes irrelevant to the theory's concepts and propositions. In this case, we are saying that different methods should not produce different conclusions; if they do, these differences become theoretically relevant and must be reconciled.

If methods produce different findings, we may be learning more about the methods

[10] Eugene J. Webb, Donald T. Campbell, Richard D. Schwarta and Lee Sechrest, *Unobtrusive Measures: Non-Reactive Research in the Social Sciences* (Skokie, Ill.: Rand McNally and Co., 1966).
[11] Scott Greer, *The Logic of Social Inquiry*, p. 56.

than about the problem we are trying to solve. An example of this is the dispute between persons who study 'community power' through a reputational approach (asking knowledgeable people who have power in their city) and 'issue analysis' (determining who participates in selected community decisions). These two methodologies produced consistently different results. Insofar as theorists claim to be talking about the same thing, this is disturbing and makes both theories questionable. The reputational approach turned up a much smaller, more centralized elite than did the issue approach. The discrepancy has produced many attempts at theoretical reconciliation (power behind the scenes, etc.) on the one hand, and methodological concern on the other; does the reputational method itself (by asking for a list of top people) make the finding of such a group inevitable? That is, are the findings an artifact of the methodology rather than a true description of community power? This is like saying the experimental situation and not the seminars produced the positive responses.

If various approaches to a problem produce consistent findings, however, this is very encouraging. We have tried still another approach to falsification and failed.

The research cycle is the vehicle through which theories are continually reexamined, rejected, or modified to more closely account for the data. All interested persons have access to the process in order that they may pose challenges to the theory. A given piece of research may rest on very limited or very extensive data, simple or complex research techniques, it may be a highly original formulation or a replication study. The researcher's responsibility is that he has sought out contrary evidence and accounted for it in his theory. His research is open to revision if future investigation produces contradictions.

For Further Reading

Devine, Richard P. and Falk, Laurence L., *Social Surveys: A Research Strategy for Social Scientists and Students,* Morristown, N. J.: General Learning Corporation, 1972.

This is an excellent discussion of the nature of social science and how students can participate in social science, including a very easy to follow discussion of the specific steps one goes through in carrying out research. It is very short and it provides a useful bibliography for further reading.

Campbell, Donald T., "Administrative Experimentation, Institutional Records and Non-Reactive Measures," in *Organizational Experiments, Laboratory and Field Research,* Wm. N. Evan, ed. New York: Harper & Row, Publishers, 1971.

This is a seminal article on the making of "Quasi-experimental" research projects. It is a version of Campbell's notions of "social reform as experiment." It is also a source for his checklist of known "threads to validity."

Habenstein, Robert W., *Pathways to Data, Field Methods for Studying Ongoing Social Organizations,* Chicago: Aldine, 1970.

A very useful guide to studying the near at hand, the local campus or community, your home town, the places where you have worked.

McCall, George J. and Simmons, J. L., *Issues in Participant Observation: A Text and Reader*.

This is a consideration of the classic formulations of this kind of research and a critical examination of the field techniques.

5 | Research Strategies

OBSERVATION

OBSERVATION is a useful way to approach a problem about which not very much is known. Actually observing a situation has a number of other advantages. It is possible to study problems or situations which people can't or won't tell you about. This includes phenomena which participants take so completely for granted that they no longer 'see' them. A mayor who has 'known' politics to be of a certain sort all his life may not think to tell you that he spends most of his time—not consulting with experts, not making decisions, not reviewing plans or proposals, not even corresponding—but talking with constituents who come to his office about a variety of human problems. Yet this is an interesting puzzle for the social scientist. The mayor's daily activities may be an important clue as to why he is powerful. Similarly, business executives have been observed to have virtually no uninterrupted time in which they might plan or make decisions—their apparent functions.[1] They devote most of their time to trying to get information—usually from subordinates—another puzzle which may be a clue for organizational theorists.

Other information which is difficult to get by questioning includes that which is embarrassing or illegal. Further, it includes information which is in some respects ephemerallike loving behavior, flirtatious behavior, or religious experience. Such occurrences may be very important for understanding a given situation, but very difficult to document, short of observation by another human being with a capacity to be sympathetic. The existence of such behavior must still be reported in terms of replicable empirical observations. Liston Pope, for example, describes religious 'sects' as having more "fervor" in their services than are found in the services of established 'churches.' He describes some of his observations:

All the while waves of ecstatic rhythm have been sweeping over the congregation, with the actions of the preacher setting the pace. There are patterns to the rhythmic actions: running around the pulpit, holding trembling hands to the sky, very fast clogging of the feet, swinging the arms in sharp, staccato motions. One

---

[1] Robert Dubin, ed. "Managerial Behaviors," in *Human Relations in Administration* (Englewood Cliffs, N. J.: Prentice-Hall, Inc., 1968), pp. 179-185.

girl leaps from her seat as though struck by an electric shock, races four times around the aisles of the church screaming 'O God . . . do Jesus . . . O God . . . glory, glory, glory . . . give me more . . . more . . . glory, glory, glory': falling backward with hands outstretched, her whole body quivering and rhythmically jerking, she collapses at last in a dull heap on the floor, and stays there in comatose condition for several minutes. Others rise and shout at the top of their lungs for five minutes, or bang on something in staccato rhythm. The same persons respond again and again, with perhaps seventy-five individuals represented. Each responds with an individual pattern of motions but all motions revolve around a few general types. The motions appear to have been culturally conditioned, whether immediately conditioned by the agent or not. One wonders if some form of mass hypnotism is at work.[2]

While interpretation is directly dependent upon carefully documented observables such as those in this study, it it greatly facilitated by the presence of an empathetic human being.[3]

This is a reason that participant observation is a favored technique where the view of the participants is held to be important to understanding a problem. By learning and coming to humanly understand the viewpoint of the local people in the Italian slum he studied, Whyte was able to put the rackets and the political machine into a very different perspective than that which was dominant.

There is a danger in this process. The observer may over-identify with the flux of ongoing human life and lose his or her research perspective. The danger of over-involvement is, of course, related to the degree of interaction between researcher and subjects. Plotting neighborhood visiting patterns on a pre-established schedule (who waved at whom, who stopped to talk on the street, who made a special visit to the home of a neighbor and so forth) need not mean any particular involvement with the subjects of the study.

Where involvement is a potential threat, the observer should take unusual (extraordinary) care to assure that field notes are as objective as possible and that the observer does not throw his or her self into the group in ways which alter its behavior (trying to influence the group, for example).

A notable value of observational research is that it allows the researcher a very extensive flexibility to pursue leads, redefine importance, and cope with unanticipated problems. This is invaluable in exploratory research. Hence observational techniques are frequently used to explore new areas, to challenge prevailing approaches, and to generate new theories.

Observational studies may be replicated to good advantage by similar studies. For example, several small studies describe similar patterns in business executives' allocation of time (minutes of uninterrupted time, minutes spent talking with subordinates, and so on). This reduces doubt that unique factors may have been at work in any one study. The more complicated and time-consuming the study, however, the less the likelihood of replication, and observational research *is* time-consuming. An observer has to be around long enough to observe recurrent patterns and have the time to carefully record and reconstruct events. Use of a tape-recorder increases the amount

[2]Liston Pope, *Millhands and Preachers* (New Haven, Conn.: Yale University Press, 1942), pp. 132-133.
[3]Max Weber called such empathizing "verstehen." The researcher asks himself: "What would it mean if I were to carry out such actions?"

of time needed, since transcribing takes a great deal of time. Moreover, a large portion of observation will be ultimately irrelevant. Further, the researcher must completely adapt his schedule to the research problem, since it can not be made to adapt to his.

These considerations severely limit the number of cases a given investigator can handle. They also limit the possibilities for a research team to operate in a consistent fashion. Observational studies are, therefore, rarely conclusive as verification. Rather, provocative theoretical propositions are extracted from these studies and verified through other approaches.

INTERVIEWS AND QUESTIONNAIRES

Interviews and questionnaires are systematic ways of asking questions of people. In an interview, the researcher or someone hired by the researcher personally questions individuals. The researcher records responses according to some plan or 'schedule' which has been worked out beforehand. The questionnaire is a schedule of questions which informants are asked to fill out themselves and return to the investigator.

Asking questions of people is very useful for problems in which it is important to know what a person is thinking. Imagine, for example, that you are a researcher who knows nothing about football. The most efficient way to uncover the logic of this coordinated human activity would probably be to ask participants what they were up to. A number of comedians have been quite successful with the technique of imagining a novice trying to understand a football game (one body of bodies crashing into another body of bodies in some relation to a ball and surrounded by screaming others) through observation alone. (Although a participant observer would join the team).

Think of other forms of human organization (the family, the military, the factory) as other games which, like football, have definitive rules. You can understand the popularity of asking questions as a rapid way of gaining information. You can see also that, if you were satisfied with the information obtained, you could cover more ground (talk to more people) than you could hope to cover as an observer.

Formal questioning may take a wide range of forms. An interviewer may begin with only a very few general questions, which he follows up with more specific questions as he learns more from the interviewee. If we imagine complete ignorance, as we did in the football example, there would likely be only one question: "What was that you were doing out there on the field this afternoon?" or "What do you understand football to be?" Usually a person conducting this sort of non-directive, 'in-depth' interview will begin with five or six general questions designed to elicit generally informative remarks which will give the researcher ideas for more questions.

Data collected in this way is not consistent for all persons interviewed, cannot be easily tabulated, and requires considerable interpretation. Its interpretation requires skills similar to those of the observer-researcher who must find patterns and exceptions to patterns in data which was not collected to be "orderly."

A very different form of questionning occurs when a respondent is asked to select a response from several clearly specified answers. In such research orderly, quantifiable data is assured. This form of questionning is appropriate in research where it is clear what variables are to be examined for relationship, where proposed relationships are to be verified or eliminated, and clear comparability among responses is necessary. This is only possible, however, when the understanding of the researcher is far enough advanced so that the questions make sense and adequately fit the situation. Irrelevant orderliness is like a pretty map which bears no relationship to the earth. We have all been asked to fill out questionnaires which don't offer the desired choice, or which inquire about things in which we have no interest, experience, or opinion.

Between the exploratory depth interview and the closed question (actually closed answer) questionnaire are many possibilities, depending upon the specifiability of research questions and the desirability of having an interviewer present. For example, an interviewer may ask each interviewee to respond to a schedule of questions which is exactly the same for each, but where the questions themselves and the interviewer's behavior allow plenty of room for new ideas to be brought up and be explored fully. A researcher might know some things about football and want each respondent to speak to these issues (What is your relationship to the quarterback? How would you feel about being traded to another team?). Yet new ideas and themes would also be noted (and possibly incorporated in the formal interview schedule). Here the interviewer would "probe" for further elaboration: "What did you mean by that?" Why do you think that is?" If the investigator wants only information on the topics he specifies, he will try to keep the interview on a more narrow course.

Questionnaires have less flexibility but can have various combinations of "open" questions (where the respondent writes his answer in a space provided) and "closed" (specified choice) questions.

Asking people questions allows a researcher to get their point of view not only in the present but also to inquire about the past and future. It has limitations insofar as people may misremember the past and poorly predict their future behavior. Insofar as research relies on what people say, it may also be filled with the misconceptions, exaggerations, and rationalizations of those questioned.

A type of "panel" interviewing grew out of a distrust of people's memories and predictions about their voting behavior. A panel study asks people only about their present behavior but asks them at various points in time. For example, a study asked a set of respondents for whom they would vote "if the election were held today?", but asked them on numerous occasions in the months preceding the election. A panel study is a good strategy when the research problem concerns changes over time, since it does not rely so much on memory and anticipation. Its use does not resolve discrepancies between what people say they will do and what they actually do.

The presence of an interviewer poses some of the same questions as the presence of an observer. What is the effect of the interviewer on the interviewee? An interviewer must be present when on-the-spot flexibility is important. In an exploratory study there is a need to be flexible in order to develop themes as seems appropriate and to go beyond original formulations. At other times an interviewer may be necessary to explain the meaning. For example, changes in wording or elaboration may be necessary in order to communicate the same meaning to different types of people. When such flexibility is essential, the size of the study tends to be limited to what one or a few well coordinated persons can handle.

When it seems that questions may appropriately be asked in a standardized fashion, a structured interview or a questionnaire may be chosen. The ways in which an interviewer affects the respondents are not well researched, but it seems that a good interviewer is socially rewarding in ways a good questionnaire is not, and therefore is more able to secure cooperation and elicit thoughtful answers. On the other hand, respondents may be more apt to give what they think is the most socially desirable answer (even when the interviewer has been careful not to give any indications that one or another answer is preferable). Persons may also be more inhibited in speaking about 'taboo' topics.

A large scale distribution of questionnaires is apt to get a poor response rate; and rarely can people be forced to comply. Hiring a large number of interviewers also poses problems. A single, self-directed interviewer can know what efforts were made to avoid influencing responses, is aware of problems encountered, knows that the interviews were conducted consistently and can, when it appears influence may have been unavoidable, take this into account in looking at responses. A large number of interviewers must be trained to behave in an appropriate and consistent fashion. Those responsible must elicit necessary feedback from interviewers and build in checks to assure that tasks are actually being carried out. Interviewers who are paid by the interview have too frequently been found to be making up the answers—particularly for those people they have trouble locating.

Such necessary precautions are very expensive. Unless these things are assured, however, increasing the size of the sample is detrimental rather than desirable. Julius Roth goes so far as to say:

I am convinced that research tasks carried out by hired hands are characterized not rarely or occasionally, but typically, by restricted production, failure to carry out portions of the task, avoidance of the more unpleasant or difficult aspects of research, and out right cheating. The results of research done in part or wholly by hired hands should be viewed as a dubious source for information.[4]

All large organizations face problems such as these. Obviating them is not only expensive in dollars, but involves considerable administrative skill.

A large scale interview study is expensive and inflexible. It must have good theory behind it, and carefully worked out questions, since it is difficult or impossible to correct for errors (like irrelevancy) after it is underway.

There are very substantial advantages, however, when such a study is properly conceived and executed. Structured questions produce data which are orderly and systematic, indeed capable of numerical presentation. If these answers have been obtained from a random sample of persons in the relevant categories, the data can be statistically manipulated in highly desirable ways. Descriptions and verification become possible on a grand scale.

[4] Julius Roth, "Hired Hand Research," *American Sociologist* (1966), p. 195.

EXPERIMENTS, QUASI-EXPERIMENTS, AND MULTI-VARIATE ANALYSIS

The experiment is the ideal in verification research. A theory has predicted that certain relationships exist. Predictions made from the theory are taken into the laboratory. Identical situations are created. All factors are held constant except the one being tested. The 'treatment' is applied to one of the two identical groups. If the predicted outcome occurs, the relationship between the 'treatment' and the outcome is confirmed. The theory is validated.

Sociology has few opportunities for true experimentation. Most of the social world cannot be brought into the laboratory without altering it beyond recognition. Further, the idea of doing so, and still more the possible means of doing so, raise serious moral questions.

The freshman seminar study, cited earlier, is an example of an experiment where the artificiality of the situation was minimal. Even there, however, the students' responses may have been affected by their being singled out for study. A better experiment was Schwartz and Skolnick's study of the effect of criminal records on future employment of unskilled workers. These researchers prepared employment folders for workers which were identical in every respect except one: the stated criminal record. These folders were sent to potential employers who did not know of the experiment. The researchers' compared criminal record differences with the employer's receptivity to employing the individual described in the folder. They found that employers were negative not only about convicted criminals but about those individuals who had been indicted but found innocent. Their speculations about the relationship between known indictment and employment were confirmed.[5] Furthermore, given the structure of this experiment, there do not seem to be any rival explanations of similar plausibility.

This is a kind of research which is extremely difficult and often morally questionable to attempt. Consider the researcher who told college students they were receiving psychological counselling in order to observe whether they would impute an orderliness to random pieces of advice. 1) Was it legitimate to do so? 2) Could this study be replicated with other groups in the society? 3) Should it be?

Even where morality is not an issue, the social world is so complex that 'controlling' the effect of extraneous variables is difficult. What is the cause of urban unemployment? Can we study a hypothesized 'culture of poverty' without controlling the effects of the economy? the polity? racism? Is there any way these things can be brought into the laboratory?

There are two approximations to the laboratory: quasi-experimental design and multivariate analysis. Quasi-experimental design involves taking advantage of 'natural' experiments and available data. All corrective public policy is a form of natural experimentation. So also are new programs in schools and reforms in industry. Normally, however, there are not comparable records of the pre-existing situations, the 'treatment' and the outcomes. The result is that there are many rival explanations which are plausible. After the fact it is difficult to estimate the likelihood that the particular program had a given effect or not,

[5] R. D. Schwartz and J. H. Skolnick, "Two Studies of Legal Stigma" *Social Problems* (1962).

since many other factors, elements, were uncontrolled. Thus, quasi-experimental design relies on cooperation from persons who plan and keep the records on our natural experiments. If this cooperation were forthcoming, the social world might be a less morally ambiguous laboratory.

For example, a school district might adopt a new line of textbooks, not all at once but on an experimental basis, with some schools starting on the new books and some not. These two groups of schools would be in all other respects similar (in terms of wealth and education of parents, past achievement of students, race, and so forth). The experiment should cover several years. If this were done, the effect of the books themselves could be more reliably examined.

Small scale studies replicated many times and in many places have definite advantages and most closely approximate the method which has been so successful for the physical sciences. Cooperation from those who experiment in the world anyway could contribute greatly. Short of that, social scientists must rely on what is presently possible by way of continual replication of studies and continual comparison of the findings of these studies.

Multi-variate analysis is another way of bringing the logic of the laboratory into social science research. In multi-variate analysis, a large amount of data on many attributes is collected. Then the *data* are manipulated, instead of manipulating persons in a laboratory. For example, suppose we are interested in an observed correlation indicating that absenteeism from work is greater in the case of women than it is for men. We know, however, that many factors and influences are different in the lives of men and women. We don't know which of these is responsible for the correlation we observe. The laboratory ideal would indicate that we should think of as many possible factors as we can, and vary these one by one. We would, for example, have two groups of individuals with similar jobs, of similar ages, with similar tenure and so on. The only thing different about them would be their sex: one group would be women, one group men. There would be many, many such controlled groups. All other things being equal, do the women show higher rates of absenteeism?

We imagine another experiment. This time we compare men with men or mixed groups with mixed groups, age and other factors are the same, with only job type differing. All other things being equal, does job type affect absenteeism?

Another way to do this is to collect a large amount of data and let the computer sort out these groups (who are now represented by computer cards rather than in person). First the computer sorts out those cards which represent people alike in every relevant respect except gender. Then it sorts out cards representing those alike in every respect except job type. It performs the experiments by comparing these data. Gender does not affect absenteeism. Type of job does. The spurious correlation between gender and absenteeism is explained by the concentration of women in low-skilled, low-paying jobs where absenteeism tends to be high (for whoever holds the jobs).[6]

[6]U.S. Department of Labor, "Facts About Women's Absenteeism and Labor Turnover" in Nona Glazer-Malbin and Helen Youngelson Waehrer (eds.) *Woman in a Man-Made World: A Socioeconomic Handbook* (Skokie, Ill.: Rand McNally, 1972), pp. 265-271.

Short of much replication, multi-variate analysis has obvious attractions. The data need only be collected once, after which it can be continually reanalyzed to test new hypotheses. The natural setting is preserved (we don't put people in different rooms, or tell them they are being studied and make them feel like guinea pigs).

There are dangers in this apparently easy solution however. The sample must be large if extraneous factors (like region of the country, type of job) are to be assumed as cancelling each other out (the idea of the random sample). The effect of passing time (with all that may involve) on the observed events may be lost—unless the data are, like the census, collected periodically.

Further, the dangers we discussed for large scale interviewing are obviously present. If a researcher does not collect his own data (and control his interviewers and so forth), he is dependent upon the reliability of those who did. True replication would expose such errors in a way multi-variate analysis will not. Further, the categories in which the data were collected may not be the best indicators for the present research problem. If not, there is the danger that the available data rather than the research hypothesis will define the concepts. Methodological Cargo Cuts rather than tests of suggestive theories result. A clearly responsible study of a small sample providing a partial (to be further replicated) test of a good theory is much preferable to a large study which lacks good theory or responsible methodology.

ANALYSIS OF DOCUMENTS

What documents are commonly used by sociologists? There are many different types.

Multi-variate analyses draw heavily on the many government surveys, of which the decennial census is the most important. They consult the growing archives of prior survey data collected by social scientists. The data in a survey is analyzed by its original collectors only with respect to one or a few research problems. The data in it (population characteristics, attitudes, reported behavior) may well be relevant to other research questions. Further, social scientists analyze institutional records (of, say, the military or a private industry), and sometimes the data of market or policy research units.

Data like those available in the census constitute an important source for a wide variety of research. Demographers and ecologists take the lead here in pointing up the importance of such factors as population composition. Populations are described in terms of the number of men and women in the unit, the ages of the people, the mortality rate, the birth rate, and so forth. At a glance it is clear whether a few adults of working age are supporting many children and older people, or whether many productive adults have relatively few dependents. It is often very useful to have an overall picture including such facts as these.

Another large data source is the more anthropological Human Relations Area Files, built upon many separate studies in which characteristics of hundreds of societies are recorded. Here such component facts as kinship patterns, sex roles, and religious practices are recorded and may be compared. Once again gains in scope involve the loss of control over data collection. The Human Relations Area Files include everything from missionary reports to the accounts of highly skilled observers.

There are, of course, many other sources of information which sociologists have imaginatively used. One of the earliest empirical studies is Thomas and Znaniecki's *The Polish Peasant in Europe and America*.[7] This was a study of personal correspondence between Polish immigrants in Chicago and their friends and relatives in Poland. Another sociologist studied the growth of pessimism in American Protestantism through a content analysis of a monthly religious publication.[8]

Data sources such as these can never be considered representative; but the random sample and its approximations are only necessary when the aim is verification. When a problem can best be solved by ingenuity, ingenuity is the best method.

We should probably not conclude this discussion of the research behind sociology without again mentioning the learned journals in which the research is published and shared. The beginning sociology student should become well acquainted with the *Social Sciences and Humanities Index*, a quarterly journal where the research articles which have appeared in journals are indexed by topic. It is in the comparison and criticism of published articles that sociological findings are sorted out. The organizing and teaching of this knowledge is the great contribution of many sociologists.

For Further Reading

Greer, Scott. *The Logic of Social Inquiry*. Chicago: Aldine, 1969.

A general discussion and analysis of the logic which underlie the major strategies of research used by social scientists. See in particular section IV, "A Working Definition."

Phillips, Bernard S. *Social Research, Strategy and Tactics*. New York: The Macmillan Company, 1971.

This is a sound general text on the entire research cycle. Like Greer's work, it is written for the aspiring "working social scientist."

Wiseman, Jacqueline P. and Aron, Marcia S. *Field Projects for Sociology Students*. Cambridge, Mass.: Schenkman Publishing Company Inc., 1970.

This is a very useful handbook of sociological research methods which can be read by the beginning student interested in investigating his own social environment. It covers mostly exploratory methods of field research.

Bart, Pauline and Frankel, Linda. *The Student Sociologist's Handbook*. Cambridge, Mass.: Schenkman Publishing Company Inc., 1971.

This is a most thorough coverage of what a student of sociology should know about what is available to him. It ranges from the description of the sociology paper to the nature and availability of governmentally collected data, and it informs the student precisely what he can find in a library or research center.

[7] W. I. Thomas and Florian Znaniecki, *The Polish Peasant in Europe and America* (University of Chicago Press, 1920).

[8] Thomas Hamilton, "Social Optimism and Pessimism in American Protestantism" in Paul F. Lazarsfeld and Morris Rosenberg, eds. *The Language of Social Research* (New York: The Free Press, 1955), pp. 213-217.

6 | Social Science and Social Life

THE reader may by now have grown confused from too many trips around the research cycle, and may ask himself: What has this got to do with me? One answer is that he is inspecting the workshop in which, increasingly, we create social fact. We have noted that fact is "intellectually formulated event." That formulation becomes increasingly important as time-honored formulae for social life cease to work, as the social world becomes more complex and we see that custom will not do. Thus the social sciences become crucial, not in proportion to their accuracy as describers and predictors, but in proportion to the gravity of the problems confronting us.

We have already noted the early development of astronomy and mathematics. Each was based on dramatic regularities easily observed, but each was also of great social importance. Astronomy developed, not just as a pure science of the heavenly bodies, but as a way of foretelling the future, of making decisions about social life. When the priest-kings of Chaldea went to the top of the ziggurat, a man-made mountain in the flat Mesopotamian landscapes, they went to commune with the gods, and they returned to the people with the words of the gods. Astrology and astronomy grew up together, one a religious technology, the other a science.

And in another, independently developed urban society, the heavenly bodies were of great consequence. The Aztecs also created man-made mountains bringing them closer to the gods.

"The individual Mexica acquired with his very mother's milk a sense of collective mission in a world balanced upon the edge of destruction. From their predecessors in Middle America the Mexica inherited the concept of worlds created and consumed in recurrent cataclysm. . . . In the great war to uphold the cosmos, the Mexica saw themselves as fighters on the side of light, sun, valor, courage, sobriety, and sexual control against the forces of night, earth, cowardice, drunkenness, and sexual incontinence. Only continuous warfare and human sacrifice could maintain the sun in its heaven; only continuous military effort could postpone that final day when the present cycle of events would draw to an end, when the world would disintegrate in a cosmic cataclysm."[1]

For the Aztec (Mexica in Wolfe's term) the sun was in danger of being devoured by the stars of night, and only human blood

[1] Eric Wolf, *Sons of the Shaking Earth* (University of Chicago Press, 1959), pp. 144-145.

could keep back the horde of stars. Thus there was concern with the heavens; what could be more important?

I am not suggesting that the social fact upon which the Aztecs based their social policy was correct. Indeed, it exposed the empire to enormous internal pressure, making it easy prey for the invading Spaniards. But the point is this: it *was* the governing fact and from it developed far-reaching, important consequences. It would have paid the Aztecs to have developed a philosophy with more reality-testing involved; it would have saved the lives of hundreds of thousands of sacrificed victims.

An atomic physicist recently appeared on a television program. He was one of those concerned scientists who, after the atomic bomb was developed, formed a society to try to prevent its use. He was asked what the science of physics could do to prevent World War III and a nuclear holocaust. His answer was brief: Nothing. Only the social sciences, our knowledge of human society and ability to control it, can prevent the ultimate mistake for the human race.

Thus unsure as we may be about given theories in social science, we can have no doubt as to the importance of the enterprise. Whether it is carried out on campuses, in research institutes, in government agencies, it is our equivalent of keeping the stars of night from devouring the sun and thereby bringing the world to an end. (This is also a reason to be concerned that sociological theory be as accurate as possible, so that we may not needlessly sacrifice hundreds of millions of people.)

SOME USES OF SOCIAL FACT

A first and most obvious use of social fact is in regulating everyday behavior among people. It makes a great deal of difference whether we see people of origins different from us as variations of the human species, or, in the phrase of Erik Erikson, as members of *pseudo species*. The terrible crimes against humanity committed by the Nazis were based on their belief that people who differed from them were really a different kind of animal.

But social fact is increasingly important in formulating social policy—the public response to situations conceived of as problems of the society. We should recall the discussion of heroin addiction. There it was clear that if you accepted one explanation of heroin addiction, say group norms, your policy would be very different from that which you would devise based upon another explanation—for example, the organization of the marijuana market. And whether your policy worked might very well depend upon whether you chose the correct theory of heroin addiction.

But there are even more momentous policy questions in which social science is important. Our international policies—in dealing with Russia, China, Israel, the Arab states—are not based upon physical science. They are rarely founded on common sense, the beliefs we hold in common, for there is too much variation among these. Instead, they are based upon the opinions of experts in the various cultures, among them "Kremlinologists" as they are sometimes called. To understand the way the various leaders understand what they are doing and what we are doing, we must exercise *verstehen* in as careful a way as possible. For to assume that we are all members of the human race does not exclude recognizing that we do vary significantly in our norms, values, and resulting frames-of-reference.

International relations are also much affected by the particular kinds of social fact generated by our theories. Thus it is important to the Marxist social scientist that many of his country's international neighbors are capitalist, societies based upon private ownership of the means of production. His very formulation of problems begins with a set of beliefs as to what policies this will produce in say, capitalist America. In the same way, the American social theorist, emphasizing a pluralist society in which many groups contend for the control of public policy, power and resources, tends to see the Marxist-based regimes as curious deviants from the obvious norm of a liberal-capitalist society.

While the Marxist is not apt to convert the liberal-capitalist to his point of view, or *vice versa*, it is useful that they understand each other's bias and perhaps, in the process, learn to take their own into account. It is probably an error to believe that a Marxist party-state can ever be a "friend" of a liberal-capitalist state, and the latter kind of society must always reject one in which there is only a single political party, and that one committed to the destruction of the pluralist political system. However, they can relate to each other with better information if the social scientists in each kind of society know what the adversary is up to and what he thinks it means. The reason for such knowledge is clear from the previous discussion: All men on earth have a reason for preventing the stars from devouring the sun and bringing the cosmos to an end.

Social fact is also important for policy concerning the internal social relations of a society. It is one thing to believe that poverty is the product of individual flaws in character, and another to believe that flaws in character are produced by the society. One requires that we face up to a continuing number of people who are inept, unable to cope, and who must be treated as such. (We can choose "benign neglect" or Christian charity, of course; the social fact does not *dictate* the social policy.) The other theory requires action at the level of education and opportunity. Of course we can also consider the possibility that poverty is a product of social structure, without respect to the character of the individual. Certainly the transformation of American society from a depression-land where millions were unemployed and had been for years, to the immensely productive "arsenal of democracy" in World War II, did not result from a sudden shift in social character. Instead, it came about from a massive increase in opportunity.

Whatever one's personal feelings about these matters, they rest upon assumed social fact, and these in turn are produced by the frame-of-reference and the research cycle employed by their makers. These frames-of-reference are, in the beginning, conventional wisdom, the lore of the tribe. They are handed down for generations, unexamined, acted upon as long as the results are more or less satisfactory. But they may be profoundly incorrect, as is often the belief that people from different backgrounds are of different species, and the results may be as tragic, as the fate of Afro-Americans in the United States, or Catholics in North Ireland. In modern, complex societies undergoing continuous change the probability that such lore will retain its usefulness becomes very small; man must remake his social fact as he remakes himself.

UNDERSTANDING SOCIOLOGY
Social Science and Social Life

SCIENCE AND HUMANISM

The student of society must, as we have reiterated, keep in mind the many dimensions of our experience. The social scientific vision is one that derives from abstracting, out of all the experiences we have, those which are indicators of the regularity, externality, and the constraint of human groups upon their constituent members. Some have seen this as an anti-humanistic position, one which minimizes personal freedom and the values of individuals. Science is, to them, the new barbarism.

Yet social science flourishes in the societies which are most committed to humanism, least the prey of massive totalitarian thought control. For social science is an enlightening enterprise, one which tends to diminish the hierarchy, mystery, and blind faith in authority which are cultivated by those whose main concern is control and the protection of privilege. It tends to improve our chances of governing ourselves wisely for it makes explicit the true nature of problems and the situations which produce them, allowing us wiser action.

This revelation of the nature of things is often couched in terms of the constraining effects of social structure. But the social scientists are not responsible for the constraints; those who oppose social science on the grounds that it reduces human freedom of choice are simply interested in punishing the messenger who brings bad news. And the news is frequently bad. Men are in large part limited by the very structure of their society; in a poor society nobody can be really rich. They are controlled by organizations subject to all kinds of ills, from arteriosclerosis to perpetual nervous breakdowns. (You will recognize the organismic metaphor.) And some would say, with T. S. Eliot, that humanity can only stand a little reality.

This implies a very mean view of humanity. It is our belief that it is not only more practical to "live in the truth," but it is also nobler and more conducive to the full development of the human race—whose outcome we do not know. Certainly a philosophy which systematically distorts empirical fact, which systematically blinds us to the nature of the social world, cannot be a very profound one. And in a way, the entire enterprise of humanity is engaged in improving its philosophy, so that it may improve its way of living.

For Further Reading

The student can find an extensive literature on the relationship between sociology and society. We shall limit ourselves to a few examples.

Horowitz, Irving Louis. *Sociological Self Images: A Collective Portrait.* Beverly Hills, California: Sage Publications, 1969.
 This is a candid and fascinating account, by a group of eminent sociologists, of their life in sociology. It includes essays by George Homans, Wendell Bell, Robert A. Nisbet, Seymour Martin Lipset, and others.

Snow, C. P. *The Two Cultures and the Scientific Revolution.* New York: Cambridge University Press, 1961.
 This is a lively and still controversial tract which argues that we are two cultures, humanistic and scientific, and that the humanists had better learn to understand the scientific.

Toulmin, Stephen. *The Philosophy of Science, An Introduction.* New York: Harper & Row, Publishers, 1960.
 For the beginner, this is a delightful and easily understandable introduction to the material of this book from a technical, philosophical viewpoint. It will complement the entire book and throw some light upon the questions raised in this chapter.

Glossary

Abstraction—Taking out or perceiving some and not other aspects of experience.

Analytic Induction—A research strategy in which every case that does not fit the researcher's generalizations is examined rigorously. A single negative case forces a reformulation.

Artifact—A product of artificial character due to extraneous influence.

Case—One individual or unit of investigation.

Category—A group, set, or kind sharing common attributes.

Conceptualize—Formulate experience in terms of ideas.

Connotation—The meanings suggested to an individual by a given stimulus such as a word or object.

Correlation—When a change in one variable is consistently accompanied by a change in another variable.

Cycle—A course or series of events or operations that recur regularly and lead back to the starting point.

Data—(singular: datum) information given or admitted as a basis for reasoning or inference.

Deduction—The drawing of specific conclusion about a specific event from a general knowledge of that *kind* of event.

Demographers—Persons who analyze statistically aggregate data for human populations with reference to size, distribution, age, sex, birth and death rates, and migration.

Denote—To indicate a particular object.

Deviant Case—Also called "negative case." An exception to the rule.

Empirical—Originating in or based on observation or experience; capable of being verified or disproved by observation or experiment.

(By permission from Webster's New Collegiate Dictionary © 1973 by G. & C. Merriam Co., Publishers of the Merriam Webster Dictionaries.)

Experiment, Scientific—One of two groups matched for their similarity is "treated" with an experimental variable in order to determine under controlled circumstances whether or not the treatment had the effect predicted from a theory.

Frame of Reference—A universe of discource; a connected set of "facts" and "axioms" in reference to which members of a group do their thinking, their

GLOSSARY
Continued

defining of situations, their conceiving of personal and group roles in such situations, and their communicating of such thoughts and attitudes.

Heuristic—Useful in furthering research but not necessarily having future utility.

Hypothetical—Of or depending on supposition; conjectural.

(By permission from Webster's New Collegiate Dictionary © 1973 by G. & C. Merriam Co., Publishers of the Merriam Webster Dictionaries.)

Induction—The act, process or result of an instance of reasoning from a part to a whole, from particulars to generals, or from the individual to the universal.

(By permission from Webster's New Collegiate Dictionary © 1973 by G. & C. Merriam Co., Publishers of the Merriam Webster Dictionaries.)

Instrumentation—The determination of specific observables indicating the occurrence of predicted events.

Interview—The securing of information through a conversation with an individual.

Metaphor—A figure of speech in which a word or phrase literally denoting one kind of object or idea is used in place of another to suggest a likeness or analogy between them.

(By permission from Webster's New Collegiate Dictionary © 1973 by G. & C. Merriam Co., Publishers of the Merriam Webster Dictionaries.)

Multi-variate—Many variables.

Norm—A principle of right action binding upon the members of a group and serving to guide, control, or regulate proper and acceptable behavior.

(By permission from Webster's New Collegiate Dictionary © 1973 by G. & C. Merriam Co., Publishers of the Merriam Webster Dictionaries.)

Objective—Expressing or involving the use of facts without distortion by personal feelings or prejudices.

(By permission from Webster's New Collegiate Dictionary © 1973 by G. & C. Merriam Co., Publishers of the Merriam Webster Dictionaries.)

Operationalize—Translate concepts into observable events.

Participant Observation—A type of research in which the researcher attaches himself personally to a group, or institution, or type of social situation, in which to observe behavior firsthand.

Phenomenon (pl. Phenomena)—An object or aspect of an object known through the senses rather than by thought or intuition.

Practical Vision—Common sense, taken-for-granted versions of reality which are not questioned.

Problematic—Open to question or debate.

(By permission from Webster's New Collegiate Dictionary © 1973 by G. & C. Merriam Co., Publishers of the Merriam Webster Dictionaries.)

Qualitative—Of, relating to, or involving quality or kind (Qualitative research identifies components but does not use standards of precise measurement).

Quantitative—Expressable in terms of quantity. (Quantitative research examines specific variables, the attributes of which can be counted or measured and compared for their 'quantity'.)

Questionnaire—A form or schedule used for collecting data from persons who respond to questions without the assistance of an interviewer.

Random Sample—A sample in which each individual or unit in the category has an equal chance of being included.

Raw Data—Observations which have not yet been ordered or analyzed.

Replication—Repeated observation of situations theoretically the same as earlier situations studied though differing in various particulars.

Research Cycle—The process through which scientists create and test theories.

Sample—A selection of cases which is smaller than the larger category from which it is drawn.

Schedule—Collection form sheet, card, or booklet designed for recording research data.

Sense Data—Belonging to the sensible world and being intersubjectively observable or verifiable.

Social Fact—According to Émile Durkheim, refers to those regularities in social life which are *external* to the individual and *constraining* upon his actions.

Social Policy—The social response to situations conceived of as problems of the society.

Symbol—Any object or event evoking conceptual meaning.

Tentative—Not final.

Variable—Any trait, quality, or characteristic which can vary in magnitude in different individual cases. Also called variate. Used in contradistinction to attribute and to constant.

"Verstehen"—The use of human empathy to understand the actions of others in the context of research.

Index

abstraction
   levels of, 8
   selective, 9
   and value, 7
Aristotle, 1
Aron, Marcia S., 52
artificiality, 49
assumptions of science, 6
Aztec religion, 53

Bart, Pauline, 52
Becker, Howard S., 33-34
Bell, Wendell, 56
Blan, Peter, 21
bureaucracy, 12

Campbell, Donald T., 27, 37, 41, 42, 43
capitalism, 55
Clark, Cameron, 32
coerciveness, 10
concept,
   measurement of, 17
conception, 7
   of heroin addiction, 16
connotation, 7
Cottrell, Fred, 21
culture,
   and science, 7
   and symbols, 7
   and truth, 7

Darwin, Charles, 11
data,
   "hard," 26
   "soft," 26
deduction, 14
denotation, 7
Devine, Richard, 41-42, 43
documents, analysis of, 51-52
Dubin, Robert, 44
Durkheim, Emile, 10, 21

Erikson, Erik, 54
evolution, social, 12
exchange theory, 21
experimental design, 35-39, 49-50
experiments, intellectual, 6, 27
exploration, 14, 19, 26-29
   plausible, 16, 49
   rival, 14-15, 39, 41
extrapolation, 16
externality, 10

facts,
   and frame of reference, 7
   social, 10
Falk, Lawrence L., 41-42, 43
falsification, 6, 14, 27-28
   methods of, 40-43
field notes, 31
folk thought, contrasted with social science, 2
frame of reference, 7
   and abstraction, 7
   and culture, 7
   differences in, 8
   and the irrelevant, 9
   and policy problems, 55
Frankel, Linda, 52
Freud, Sigmund, 27

generality, 27
generic problems of science, 5
Glazer-Malbin, Nona, 50
Greer, Ann Lennarson, 35
Greer, Scott, 11, 26, 42, 52
groups, 11
guiding metaphors, 11-12, 20-21

Habenstein, Robert W., 43
Hamilton, Thomas, 52
Homans, George, 56
Horonity, Irving Louis, 56
hired hand research, 48

Hughes, Everett, 31-34
Human Relation Area Files, 51-52
hypothesis, 17, 19, 36

induction, 14, 32
instrumentation, 37-39
interviews, 46-48
issue analysis, 43

Lipset, Martin Seymour, 56
Langer, Suzanne, 8, 9, 11
law, 23
Lazarsfeld, Paul, 23

materialism, 21
Marx, Karl, and Marxism, 21, 55
McCall, George, 43
measurement, 17, 26
   multiple strategy, 34-35, 38-39
methods,
   choice of, 24-26
   of falsification, 40-43
   triangulation, 42-43
Merton, Robert K., 21
Mill, John Stuart, 10
misplaced concreteness, fallacy of, 10
multi-variate analysis, 50-51

Nisbet, Robert A., 56
norms of science, 2-3, 14

observation, 14, 17-18, 19
   as a research strategy, 44-46
operationalization, 17, 36

panel studies, 47
participant observation, 19, 28, 30-35, 45
Phillips, Bernard, 52
policy problems, 21, 34, 55
Pope, Liston, 44-45
practical vision, 9
   and science, 9
prediction. *See* hypotheses.
problems,
   generic, 5
   policy, 3-4
   social philosophy, 4-5
pretest, 38
professional community, 2, 19
publicity. *See* 'norms of science'.

qualitative research, 26
quantitative research, 26
Quasi-Experimental Design, 49-50

replication, 40-43, 45, 51
reputational method, 43

research cycle, 6, 13-23, 43
   an example, 15-22
   and policy, 55
research reporting, 19
reversibility. *See* 'norm of science'.
Rosenberg, Morris, 23
Roth, Julius, 48

sampling, 17
   random, 39, 52
Santayanna, George, 10
Schwartz, Richard D., 29, 42, 49
scientific method. *See* research cycle.
science,
   assumption of, 6
   as a craft, 2
   and the division of labor, 9
   nature of, 2
   norms of, 2, 14
   and practical vision, 8
   and the problematic, 1
   as process, 5, 13-14
Seechrist, Lee, 29, 42
Simmons, J. L., 43
Skolnick, J. H., 49
Snow, C. P., 56
social action theory, 21
social fact, 10, 53, 54, 55
social philosophy, problems of, 4-5
Social Sciences and Humanities Index, 52
social scientist, 2, 53, 54, 55, 56
social work, contrasted with sociology, 1
socialism, contrasted with sociology, 1, 55
sociological,
   position, 1
   thinking, 1
sociological proposition, 5-6
sociology
   practical vision, 9
Spencer, Herbert, 11
statistical analysis, 39
   significance, 39
symbolic interactionism, 21
symbols, 8
   and culture, 7
   presentational, 8

testing, 14, 17, 19
theory
   nature of, 10
   as a map, 13, 18, 19
   Grand, 21
Thomas, Wil., 52
Tomlin, Stephen, 56
Triangulation of Methods, 42-43

U.S. Census, 51

validity, 39
   threats to, 40
verification, 14, 26-29, 52
Verstehen, 54

Wallace, Walter, 21, 23
Webb, Eugene J., 29, 42
Weber, Max, 21, 27
Whitehead, Alfred North, 1, 10, 11

Whyte, William Foote, 25-26, 27
Winch, Robert F., 27
Wiseman, Jacqueline P., 52
Wolfe, Eric, 53-54

Youngelson, Helen, 50

Znaniecki, Florian, 52